Lost and Found

I am here. I am close.
I still love you.
Breathe in the love.

Lost and Found

A MOTHER CONNECTS-UP WITH HER SON IN SPIRIT

Sheri Perl

PERL PUBLICATIONS

This book is set in 11-point Adobe Jenson Pro
Design and composition by Brad Walrod/Kenoza Type, Inc.

Library of Congress Control Number: 2011917595

Library of Congress subject headings
Spiritualism
Consciousness
Lightning Source (Firm)

ISBN 978-0-9846665-0-8

First Edition

Printed in the United States of America

1 3 5 7 9 10 8 6 4 2

For Dan

CONTENTS

The Investigation Continues

Connecting-Up

INTRODUCTION

My Only Solace

I lost my son Danny on July 1, 2008 to an overdose of alcohol and prescription drugs. He was 22 years old, a beautiful mountain of a kid with his whole life ahead of him, gone in an instant due to an error in judgment.

In the last two and a half years since that harrowing day in July when his father and I discovered him, I have been on a mission to find Danny through any means available to me. In the following chapters I will walk you down the roads I have explored in my search for Dan, all which have led me to one conclusion: Danny exists! Minus his physical body, everything that I know to be true about Danny from his inner strength to his humorous personality exists. Although he is no longer here with me in physical reality, he has by no means been erased from the universe. He has made his presence known in so many ways, through so many different means that I would be in denial not to accept the validity of Danny's continued existence.

The implications of what I have just said are huge, for if Danny has survived death, then so has your loved one and for that matter, so will you. I know that's quite a statement to make, but my own experience with the realm of spirit is not new but dates back to 1971, prior to which time I was a total non-believer myself. Truth be told, had I not lived through an amazing spiritual healing experience in 1971, no one could have convinced me of the realities that I will present in this book. However, the fact remains that after four years of debilitating illness, invisible forces had such a profound impact on my health that I came to believe in the presence of invisible things. I was twenty years old when I embarked on an odyssey to learn everything that I could about those invisible forces that had healed me. At the time I was simply fascinated and wanted to know. Thirty-seven years later, after Danny passed, it was that knowledge that would save me from agonizing pain because I knew how to connect-up with Danny in the next world.

As far as I am concerned there are no words or form of comfort that can ease the pain of loss like a good connect-up and by that I mean some form of communication between yourself and your loved one in spirit. Connecting-up can be accomplished in many different ways and is not limited to sitting with mediums, although I do find great comfort in the "Interstellar Telephone," my pet name for connecting-up through a sincere and competent medium. But in whatever way you do this, be it through direct communication, (which is possible for all of us) or through another's abilities, connecting-up is the only real solace because it allows you to maintain a communication with your loved one. Instead of dwelling in memories of the past you begin to cultivate something infinitely better: an ongoing present-time relationship with your loved one on the other side.

Of course, it's not the same kind of relationship. You can't see them and you can't hug them. You can, however, still be connected-up to them because the essential energy that once looked out at you through their eyes has not been annihilated.

In the following pages you will read about the experiences that have convinced me that human experience does not end at the grave and that relationships between loved ones separated by the veil of death are both possible and natural and afford the bereaved much solace. In fact, the only real solace I know.

FOREWORD

An Overview of My Personal History and What Led Me to Discover the Spirit Realm—My Eyes Are Opened To the Presence of Invisible Things

I grew up in the 1950s in the affluent town of Short Hills, New Jersey. Although my parents, practical and logical people, created a loving environment for my siblings and me, ours was a home devoid of spirituality or mysticism of any kind. By the time I was a teenager in the mid 1960s, I was convinced that there was the "real world" in which I had my existence, and that everything outside of that was simply fantasy. The fairy tales that filled my childhood dreams were left behind along with the concept of miracles. I remember accepting this colorless interpretation of life in my early adolescence, and along with it came a sense of sadness. However, to my mind, real was real, and I prided myself on knowing the difference!

When I was afflicted with Crohn's Disease, (a chronic disease that attacks the small and large intestine) at age sixteen, my parents and I looked to medical science alone for our direction. Traditional medical science was part of the "real world" that we trusted. We placed all of our hopes on my doctors to supply us with a cure. Little did we know that from 1967 to 1969 my disease would grow in severity while we pursued medical treatment to the exclusion of all else.

It's interesting to note that I had heard of my spiritual healer as early as 1968, when I had been suffering with Crohn's Disease for a little over a year. A business associate of my father's told me about a British spiritual healer named Harry Edwards, who was known to "heal" people from a distance. I baulked at the idea and honestly felt that it was complete and utter nonsense.

By the summer of 1969 I had descended into the depths of hell, suffering more from this debilitating disease than I had ever conceived possible. At the same time I contracted Hepatitis C from blood transfusions administered during one of two emergency surgeries. By the fall of 1970 I was living with a compromised and deficient bowel system when the Hepatitis C began to surface bringing about a huge drop in my energy level as well as flu-like symptoms. Eventually medical testing revealed that I had Chronic Hepatitis. I was dumbfounded to comprehend that I had yet another disease with the potential to become more severe over time. My doctors encouraged my parents to give money to research because they believed that in the absence of a cure, I would not live past another ten years. This prognosis was made in 1971.

What happened next was that desperation paved the way to an open mind. I was not yet twenty years old and I didn't want to accept the negative prognosis that my doctors described. Neither did my father, who hired a medical student to research the illness in the hope of uncovering someone, doing something that our doctors didn't know about. I, for lack of anything else to do, started reading.

I had never been an avid reader but when my mother handed me a book titled, "The Search for Bridey Murphy" I was riveted. This book about a past life recalled through hypnosis, was the first book I couldn't put down. The book made mention of the late psychic Edgar Cayce, known as the "sleeping prophet" and again, I was seduced.

I devoured the Cayce books. A turning point in my thinking came after I read one particular Cayce case history. In this amazing story, Cayce was consulted by the parents of a young girl, who was behaving irrationally. When her medical doctors suggested an institution, the parents sought an opinion from Cayce.

Cayce, who would lie down and seemingly take a nap, would speak from a trance state, diagnosing problems and prescribing cures. In this case Cayce said that the girl had a wisdom tooth impinging on a nerve in her brain and that extraction of the tooth would make her well again. As I read on, I was excited to learn that he had been correct and the girl's health had been restored.

My first reaction after reading this was to feel sorry for myself that Edgar Cayce was no longer alive and could not shed light on my own problems. Then, from seemingly out of nowhere, came the memory of what I had heard in 1968 about the man who healed people from a distance. I started thinking, and my mind started analyzing. I thought about the Cayce story and about the fact that Cayce was lying in his bed while part of his mind was able to see into that little girl's mouth. "How could he do that?" I wondered. "Did that mean that part of Cayce was mobile and not limited to his body?" This opened up all kinds of questions and although I still lived in the "real world" I was no longer the girl who thought she knew so much about life. I decided to try to find this mysterious British healer. I had nothing to lose.

We made inquiries and my father, who was traveling to England on business, offered to hand-deliver my letter to Mr. Edwards, which was all that was required of me. Two days later, prior to my father's return, prior to reading one word on the subject of spiritual healing, I had so much energy I was flying. I just couldn't get over it. I was experiencing an overwhelming amount of energy in a body that had been weak and exhausted for years! There was no doubt in my mind that something was happening because I could feel it. Along with experiencing this incredible energy, I had a tingling sensation present all throughout my right side, in the liver area.

For a young woman who had been sick for four years, this was a new and wonderful feeling. I was not only energized physically but I was also uplifted emotionally, as if imbued with a new, strong sense of optimism. I had never experienced anything remotely like this in all my twenty years of living. For over four years I had been dragging myself around from one doctor to another and my health problems had gone from bad to worse. It was hard to believe that all I did was write a letter to Harry Edwards. This certainly did not fit into my former picture of the "real world." But to my delight, that world was crumbling in the presence of this experience. If I wasn't living through it myself I don't think I would have believed it, but it was happening to me and it was the best thing that had ever happened to me.

Within weeks of that night, my blood tests showed dramatic improvement for the first time in six months. Over the next six-month period my physical health was restored and my quest for spiritual understanding began.

The first thing I wanted to know was how the "healing" took place. I was still in wonderment about how Harry Edwards could have made this healing come about. It still seemed pretty far-fetched to me and I was even more surprised to learn from reading his book that Mr. Edwards only credited himself with a small part in the healing, that of being the messenger. He credited the greater part of the healing to spirits, who he referred to as "spirit doctors." According to Harry, it was these spirits who were responsible for carrying out the healing. This really took me by surprise since I wasn't sure I believed in spirits. Still, I could not dismiss the experience of energy that came to me from out of nowhere and turned my health and the direction of my life around for the better.

Harry explained that time and space, as we know them, do not exist in the spirit realm which makes it possible for a spirit to be any where in no time. This explained how the healing could have reached me although Harry and I were separated by the Atlantic Ocean. Because my healing experience had demonstrated to me the presence of unseen energy, I could now imagine that within that unseen energy there could be a world of spirit. I could think of no other explanation for the healing that had taken place in my body, nor did I have any reason to mistrust this incredible man, Harry Edwards, who had done more for me than all the king's horses and all the king's men, and we had some pretty top horses and men in our camp!

From that point on my eyes were wide open to endless possibilities. If spiritual healing energy directed from spirit beings was a true phenomenon, and from my experience it seemed to me that it was, then that meant that death was not an end but a continuation into spirit. What a relief to think that we are not just erased from the universe at the point of our physical death and that there actually is a plan that extends beyond physical experience.

And so in 1971 I began my investigation of that invisible world of spirit. I started out by reading Harry Edwards's books on spiritual healing and through them I was introduced to the phenomenon of mediumship. Now for the second time in my young life, I was swept away by an idea. It was thrilling for me to conceive of a world of spirit where we all went when we passed, but now I was learning that some people could actually communicate with people in that world and that they were called mediums.

Initially I read about British mediums and was impressed by the work of Jack Webber ("The Mediumship of Jack Webber"), Grace Cooke (the author of the large collection of White Eagle Books), and Leslie Flint ("Voices In The Dark"). I devoured every word of those books, amazed to discover that these mediums all worked differently in one way or another. Where Grace Cooke's work focused on bringing through the words of one communicator known as White Eagle, Leslie Flint would bring through various spirits whose voices were heard in their own dialect. Jack Webber, whose séances in dark rooms were photographed through infrared photography, also known as Kirlian photography, brought objects through his wrist into physical reality. I learned that this was called "apportion." I would never have believed any of this, however the Jack Webber book was written by Harry Edwards himself, who took part in all of the events he wrote of. I simply had to conclude that perhaps it was true that truth was stranger than fiction!

I was fascinated, but after a time I became frustrated with merely reading about mediums and spirit communication. I longed to meet a medium and to experience this phenomenon first-hand. You can imagine my thrill when I learned of a medium named Jane Roberts who spoke for a spirit named Seth and actually held weekly classes in her home, which was located twenty-five minutes from where I was living in upstate New York.

I wasted no time in contacting Jane and I started attending her ESP classes in 1974. Seth would come through Jane in every class and lecture the students on his unique perspective of life both on earth and in the realm of spirit. I was simply fascinated with this weekly demonstration of life after death, as well as Seth's perspective regarding the power of our own thoughts and beliefs to shape our lives. By the time Jane stopped holding regular weekly classes in the late 1970s I no longer doubted that the spirit world was real or that there were people called mediums who were able to communicate with beings in that world.

I could write a book about all the different mediums I have sat with over the years, and the varied ways in which they each work, however, the focus of this book is not about mediums, but about losing Daniel and finding Daniel through spiritual portals, of which mediums are one. I have included this personal history however, because I want you to know that I have been investigating mediums and the spirit realm for over four decades and that it is only after years of communicating with loved ones on the other side, that I am convinced of their ongoing existence. It is a confidence that I have gained after years of investigation and that is why I want to share it with you. But don't take my word for it. You can do your own investigating. After you read about some of my experiences with Dan, you may just want to try it!

Endings and Beginnings

CHAPTER ONE

Danny

Danny came into the world on October 22, 1985 through a birth mother who wasn't going to keep him and into the arms of Jerry and I who were seeking to adopt our second child. We had adopted our first son Aaron four years prior, an October baby as well, and so when we received a call that our baby had been born in a hospital in San Antonio, Texas, we made immediate plans to fly out and meet him the next day. That afternoon however, the hospital called us back to say that there was a problem with his respiration, implying that this baby might not be well and that we should wait and see what developed over the next few days. Jerry, however, was adamant. "He's our boy and he needs us." We took Aaron to stay with my mother and flew out to Texas.

When we laid eyes on Danny for the first time he was lying on his back in a diaper wearing dark glasses to shade his eyes from the bilirubin lights. He looked like a little man sunning himself without a care in the world. He was however, inside a glass isolate with an I.V. in his arm and frankly, I didn't know what to do. Jerry turned to the nurse nearby. "Can we take him out of there?" he asked. "Sure," she answered, and so Jerry pulled over a chair.

"Sit down Sheri," he said, and a few seconds later Jerry put Danny in my arms for the first time. It took only a moment of holding him in my arms for my maternal heart to claim this boy as my own and to commit to loving him for the rest of my life.

Of course we wanted to understand what was going on with him physically. We were told that in case of an infection he was receiving an antibiotic, however no one really understood the reason why his body was not breaking down gases properly. There was a monitor registering something to do with his respiration rate and the numbers on the monitor ranged between 80 and 100. As is common in these situations, we became fixated on watching the numbers on the monitor, without knowing what they indicated. Finally, Jerry asked the nurse what the numbers should be reading and she answered "Between 40 and 60." Now this I remember as if it were yesterday. Jerry looked into Danny's eyes and he said, "Daniel, you have a mother and a father and a brother and we are not leaving Texas without you, so calm down son, we're here!" He repeated this to Danny numerous times. Believe it or not, within thirty minutes the numbers on the monitor had adjusted to range between 40 and 60!

A few days later all three of us boarded a plane for New York to begin our family life together. Daniel grew into a bright and beautiful child who also possessed a stubborn streak and a strong propensity towards mischief. From early on I was challenged by this little boy, who could outlast, outwit and outrun me at every stage of the game. Until his diagnosis of ADHD at about age seven, I carried a lot of guilt about his behavior, thinking that it was my fault for being a soft parent. Dan wasn't a bad kid, actually he was a sweetheart, but he did what he wanted to do, period.

By the teen years we were in a quandary. Danny was heavily into drinking and smoking. He was hanging around with older kids, coming home intoxicated and worrying us terribly. Jerry would say, "We will see him in the morgue one day if we don't do something about this. This child is at risk!" We both knew it was true and so we looked for programs that we thought could help him.

We began to look into wilderness programs and emotional growth boarding schools in Oregon and Utah, the best programs we could find. It was very painful for all of us because Danny desperately wanted to stay home. I was sad all the time he was away, but we believed that we were helping him. To help us all to deal with the separation, Jerry, me, and our daughter Jessica would fly out to see him every six weeks, and Aaron, who was in college at the time, joined us whenever he could. The visits were always highly emotional. Jessica, who we adopted when Dan was seven, was the love of his life and everything from the hellos to the goodbyes broke my heart. We kept trying to believe that the programs would help Danny to gain some understanding of his emotions and some control over his actions. After four years in the program, he was sent back to us. His unhappiness at being away from home and his resistance to the programs themselves, had finally gotten him set free. "Okay," we thought. "We'll try it again at home."

Dan settled back into his own unique lifestyle. He made it through high school by the skin of his teeth, with the aid of many kind teachers who loved him and wanted to see him graduate. But he took none of it seriously and lived for the high times. He loved his little sister, our family, our dogs and his friends, but he had no desire to take on challenges and we were always very concerned about his lack of motivation. It wasn't important to us that Dan follow any particular path, but we hoped that he'd find something he felt interested in exploring, for his own fulfillment.

Looking back, it is apparent to me that despite all the doctors and programs that we pursued, no one ever fully grasped Dan's problems well enough to figure out how to help him. There is no question that he lived with anxiety and frustration, but we didn't seem able to help him either. Jerry and I came from the school of soft love, coming of age as we did, in the 1960s. When we came to see that our method of soft love wasn't getting results, we tried to take our lead from the programs he attended by letting them dictate policy.

I am glad that by the last few years of Danny's life, I had no more heart for tough love and simply told Dan that I loved him. However, as much as I would like to believe that "All you need is love," Danny's last years on earth were filled with ups and downs. We would see bursts of energy and work effort plummet into two to three days of staying in his room and not interacting with anyone, if he could help it. And then there was the partying, which was laden with laughing, good times, and frightening overindulgence. Sometimes he would tease me and say, "Sheri, I'm going to do crack cocaine!" He appeared to derive some real pleasure from letting me know that he was not going to be controlled by anyone. After I'd give him the look he'd say, "What . . . are you scared I'm going to O.D.?" to which I would answer, "Well, it could happen Dan."

And it did. It was the summer of 2008 and we were relocating to Manhattan. Our daughter was going to be finishing high school on the upper west side, and Jerry was tired of commuting. Jerry gave Danny an apartment in one of our buildings, which was located between Jerry's office on 134th street in Harlem and our new apartment on 99th street. Dan was excited to have a place of his own for the first time and agreed to work in Jerry's real estate office with his brother Aaron and the rest of the staff. I do believe that in many ways he wanted to do this, but at the same time he questioned his ability to function in an office environment.

Dan stayed stuck in his old pattern of working hard for a few days and then not showing up for a few days. We were used to this routine and so it did not strike us as odd when he didn't come into work on the morning of Tuesday, July 1st. As the noon hour rolled around we started calling him on his cell phone, however, Danny had a history of not picking up his phone and so again we assumed that Dan had had a big night. By 2:30 P.M. however, Jerry and I began to experience an uneasy feeling and we headed over to Danny's apartment. Jerry had a key of course, but the door was bolted shut from the inside. As Jerry began to kick the door in, my heart sank. I think at this point we both were preparing for the worst. When the door finally opened, we rushed in to find Danny sitting up in his bed, dead. No no no no no no no no no no no . . . it can't be! We dropped down to our knees beside him, rubbing him, begging, pleading, crying, wishing, agonizing. All of these feelings imploding at once, fighting with reality to make it not so, but we knew in our hearts the truth . . . Danny was gone.

The first person we called was Aaron who appeared almost immediately and handled the police and many of the details for us so that we could leave. He was masterful in supporting us, even though his heart was also broken. As we descended the stairs to go down to the street it occurred to me that Jerry and I were together the first time we laid eyes on this boy, and now here we were, together again when we found him.

CHAPTER TWO

The First Days Following Our Discovery of Dan—Setting Up a Prayer Team—Hearing Thoughts That Sound Like Dan—My First Glenn Dove Session

The first few days following our discovery of Dan were the hardest. I think the agony is the greatest at the beginning, before your mind has fully accepted the inevitable and rails against all logic to invent another outcome. The image comes to mind of an ice cube trying not to melt on a hot day! You can't stop the melting but you resist it, which invokes enormous suffering as your mind wrestles with reality. For me there is sadness and a sense of failure in resignation, however, it's less excruciating and exhausting than the mental struggle to un-write the written.

On that first night after finding Dan in his apartment, I crawled into bed. I was exhausted and drained and heartbroken. I was moved however, to take out my computer and send out a mass email contacting everyone in my address book. Between friends, family and all the people who at one time or another had contacted me for spiritual healing, the list was sizable. My email briefly stated that my son Danny had passed of an overdose and asked everyone to send him a prayer. I then forgot about it as the next day found us knee deep in funeral arrangements. Although

I am an interfaith minister, Jerry and I both come from Jewish families. At the time of Dan's passing we were members of a synagogue in Hastings-on-Hudson, New York, and so we naturally turned to our roots. This meant that we would have a Jewish funeral, which meant that all the arrangements had to be made immediately! I can't say that I understand this, but in Jewish tradition the body is buried within a few days of passing and so there we were, making decisions we never wanted to make, in a hurry. It was an agonizing, insane and unreal time. I must again mention Aaron who painstakingly worked out many of the arrangements for us, right down to buying Danny a new suit to be buried in.

Needless to say, the next few days were a haze of surreal events that I moved through in shock, grief and disbelief; underscored by a pervasive sense of guilt, because I had failed to protect my child. The guilt was excruciating, and gnawed away inside of me. I think I would have just beat myself up mercilessly, however right from that first day, precisely at moments of agonizing guilt, I thought I heard Dan talking to me inside my head. I would hear the words in my own voice but I would hear words that were comforting. "Mom" I would hear in my mind, "This wasn't your fault. I did it, not you. Don't beat yourself up. There was nothing you could have done," and I'd feel better for all of about 10 seconds, until I decided that it was merely my imagination.

I could have gone on giving myself a very hard time for a very long time, but the thoughts continued to come into my mind. I would hear these thoughts when I was extremely upset and they always calmed me down considerably. I remember thinking that listening to what I was hearing inside my own mind was more comforting than talking to anyone and that if I could just accept the thoughts as real, I would be able to heal a little. The problem was, I didn't think the thoughts were real and I always slipped back into a dark place. But those thoughts were persistent. I could be thinking, "You should have known, you should have called and woke him," when almost immediately I'd hear something like, "But Mom, you couldn't have known, I didn't even know," and that I believed to be true. I do not think that Danny expected the mixed-drug reaction to take his life. Of course, I couldn't know if these thoughts were coming from Dan or my own inner mind, but wherever they were coming from, they were both sane and kind.

Within the next few days, as my head cleared a little, I realized that what I needed to do was to make an appointment with the medium Glenn Dove. By this time I had been having private sessions with Glenn for fourteen years and I had come to rely on his incredible gift of mediumship to connect-up with my father, Herman Perl, and my healing guide, Harry Edwards. Over the years my respect for Glenn both as a human being and as a medium has grown and I value his friendship and his contribution to my life more than I can say. I wasn't sure if it was too soon after Dan's passing for him to come through to me, but I felt certain that at the very least, my father and Harry Edwards would, and that they would give me information about Dan.

Without mentioning that I had lost a son, I called Glenn Dove's office and scheduled an appointment at his earliest convenience, which, due to a cancellation, was in less than a week. Danny had passed on the 1st of July and I had managed to pull off an appointment for the 8th. My daughter Jessica, who was fifteen at the time, joined me. We were driven out to Glenn's office on Long Island by a close friend, also a bereaved parent, who kindly offered to escort us.

Almost as soon as the session began, Danny came through with my father. Following are excerpts from the session that took place on July 8, 2008. Present in the room was Glenn Dove, my essica Migdol and myself. I want to point out that the on completely concurred with what we already knew to ome of those facts are:

1 Danny passed of a mixture of alcohol and prescription drugs.
2 I had set up a huge prayer team for Danny
3 Danny's favorite person in the whole world was his little sister Jessica.
4 Jessica was due for a birthday on July 28th.
5 We had recently moved into the city, we were staying temporarily at my husband's office/apartment, and we were soon moving into a new apartment.
6 Jessica was starting a new school in the city.
7 Danny had never met my father who passed before Danny was born. Danny had seen my father's portrait every day because it hung in our home.
8 Danny was reckless.
9 Danny loved his car.
10 On the day before the evening he passed he had a talk with his father who told him that he was playing "Russian Roulette."

First Glenn Dove Session—
Sheri and Jessica—July 8, 2008

GLENN: There is someone over on the younger side...

SHERI: Yes.

GLENN: Because there's an untimely passing. Hold on one second. Your dad's behind him and points to his head. Someone was having a real hard time mentally. I'm not clear mentally, is what it is.

SHERI: Yes.

GLENN: And this has just happened.

SHERI: Yes!

GLENN: Oh, this is just...

SHERI: Yes, very recent.

GLENN: Cause he's telling me "Now." This is really weird, because yesterday, I believe your father tried coming to me because I was sensing somebody, and I kind of felt it was him, and he was trying to bring this younger male to me. I don't understand whether somebody had a head issue, because he's pointing to here and here. (Glenn points to his head and chest.) This is either a suicide or an accidental ... oh, I'm more confused. I don't know how clear they are because he says ... we're talking like a week or two ...

SHERI: Yes, a week ago ...

GLENN: Usually it's about six months before they can make it through.

SHERI: It's a week.

GLENN: Other than my father, who came through the night he died, most of the time it takes about six months to a year before somebody is really able to come in, but your father said it's because of him that he's coming up in front. D-A? Hold on ...

SHERI: Yes, D-A ...

GLENN: Oh, wait a second ... my God, I thought he was saying it's Dad. It's DAN?

SHERI: Yes.

GLENN: Oh my God. Okay. But he says he took his life?

SHERI: Well, I think it was accidental but I wouldn't know.

GLENN: You know, something went into his system, because that's what he's telling me.

SHERI: He took something.

GLENN: That's what it is because I feel from what comes up in front, he had an emotional imbalance. He ingested ... I get two different things going into my system and then that just led to everything that happened.

SHERI: Right.

GLENN: I don't feel a total intention, but there was a disregard for his life, the way he ran it.

SHERI: He was reckless.

GLENN: He's next to her. (Jessica)

SHERI: Of course.

GLENN: For some reason, not to be insulting to you, your father's behind you, but Dan has to sit with her. He tells me that out of anybody, it's funny you brought her today.

SHERI: It's not funny . . . this is his baby.

GLENN: Out of anybody, that's the one he has to come to. What's with the school? He says, "Do what I say, don't do what I do." He's pushing her forward. He seems okay. He seems like he's at peace on that side. I have to say that I bow down to your father because this man took the whole thing, handled the whole thing. I guess they're made aware of it ahead of time, because your father says, "There was nothing I could do about it." He didn't know your dad?

SHERI: No.

GLENN: He says, "I'm able to put people to the faces." He didn't say it but it's almost like, you put a name to the face. But he makes it seem like he knew the face but he didn't know the person. Now he goes, "I am able to put the person to the face."

SHERI: He saw pictures of them.

GLENN: Right. It took me a second as I was saying that. Um. What's the birthday?

SHERI: Her, [Jessica] birthday is July 28th.

GLENN: Your birthday's coming up. He's turning around. He wants a party for your birthday. He's going to put his humor into this. He will go into a rest period, but he said, "I'm waiting for the birthday." He wants to be around, and he sort of gives me this feeling like you better enjoy it. In other words he says, "Don't mourn this! Enjoy it." He is mentioning about a car.

SHERI: Oh, Danny's car.

GLENN: It's funny because in a way, he goes, it's almost like you figure this kid is out of the woods and he's sort of going along and all of a sudden he said, I don't want to call it a relapse but he says, he just wasn't going to get it all together in this incarnation.

SHERI: I knew that.

GLENN: And he said, he did all he was supposed to do. He could have done worse. And he says that he has a lot on that side . . . they've already told him he's going to have a lot on that side to deal with. In other words, that will be laid out for him. It's weird because I keep asking him, "Did you do this?" and he said, in an indirect way he sort of just did this to himself. I don't want to say a totally conscious way, but was this a party or something?

SHERI: Daniel's life was a party.

GLENN: God! He makes me feel like he's going to fly by the seat of his pants in life and just . . . I don't know if somebody contacted a group that pray for him, but something's been done for him and he said he's felt these waves of like, a prayer . . . a wave of prayer. He's said he's been getting these waves. He said he will go into a rest period shortly. He's hanging for the birthday. He's very protective of Jessica. It's kind of funny.

SHERI: He always was.

GLENN: I'm trying to ask if it's intentional and he says in an indirect way. It's almost like an escape because he makes me feel like I am walking down a hallway and I see an exit door and he just decides to go out the exit. It's not that he necessarily set it off, or necessarily wrote a note, but yet in the same sense, he was just playing Russian roulette with himself.

SHERI: Did he suffer?

GLENN: No. Not at all. He was just in and out. He wasn't conscious. He was just in and out. That's what happened. He wanted me to recognize it. In a way, he's a little taken back because he didn't realize the wave of . . .

SHERI: Love?

GLENN: Of everything. I can't imagine how he didn't but it's what I see with my kids; they have everything and so they don't see it. But he says to say thank you because he understands that if he asked you for the world you would have tried to give it to him and he said that he recognizes his personality as being like, you know, the rebel . . . like being the rebellious. And he said, sometimes it was uncontrollable, that he would do things and watch himself do it and not even know why he was doing it. And this is what happened at the end.

Even in passing, I've got to tell you something, it isn't like he's coming back and going "Wow, I should have." This is who he is. He'll hold true to himself. He said, "There's no one to blame." What amazes me, in the midst of all of this, is his concern for her [Jessica]. It's almost like all the things that you've instilled, which you thought went in one ear and out the other, he's now throwing on her. You guys . . . you're moving?

SHERI: Yes, we're moving again. We are staying temporarily in an apartment above Jerry's office. We will be closing soon and moving into our new apartment on 99th street.

GLENN: Okay, because he's talking about the move. He's surprised, and your father is such a help. He says that he's surprised how free he feels. Even though he's probably more in a burdened state then some other people, he says he's surprised how free he feels with everything.

SHERI: Danny?

GLENN: Yeah. It's interesting. I don't think it's something that any of us can comprehend until you experience it. We can explain what it's like to be a parent, or to be married. And I used to think I knew what it feels like. I thought, "I know what it's like to have a kid. My brother has three. I take care of my nephews." And then when I had mine it was like, "Oh my God!"

SHERI: Danny's feeling freer over . . .

GLENN: He's starting to understand the freedom and he says it's hard for us to understand because while we're still in the mortal coil, as we call it, we're not going to recognize this. I don't get the working. Was he supposed to be starting work?

SHERI: He was supposed to start working for his dad.

GLENN: Your other son is also working with him?

SHERI: The brother works for the dad too.

GLENN: Okay, because he says something about, he always saw himself below his brother. You know, you can't do that. Each kid is separate. She can't compare herself. Everybody has their own little niche. He always felt like he wasn't going to stack up, he wasn't going to add up. But this is what Danny chose in life and he says it's a whole flip and he's trying to understand it. He's okay. He said that no one's left him over there. I don't know whether you asked him because he said, whether you realize it or not, you must have said something to your dad, because no one's left his side He says, tell her . . . he makes a joke like, it's okay, you can lighten your grip . . . meaning you, because he said, "Everybody's made sure." Now, on that side, what's going to happen? Well, you can be in a confused state of mind and then your environment will reflect it but he says, "No, I just have to get my rest" and then, he said, "I will be about."

SHERI: He liked his rest.

GLENN: Yeah, he's funny like that, because he's like a sleeper. He's one of these people. It's funny because I thought he was going to say it's like a bad dream but he made me feel like this is the dream and that's the reality. What's overwhelming is his concern for his sister and his family realizing now what would happen. Sometimes, in self reflection, in one's passing, as it happens like that, you never lose consciousness. You're conscious before you're born, you're conscious during your life, and when you go over. There is never a point when you're not. But, he said, "The realism of all of it." I think it's in his self-reflecting of what his life was like, he feels that it was so short, that maybe part of his karma was in reflecting and watching it . . . seeing how he basically was handed all these things. And the other thing I need to mention, this is for you and Jerry. It wasn't like you did anything that I would say do differently. And your father is shaking his head. He said it is very important I give you that message. He said, "There's nothing you could have done that would have made any difference. He's going to try to contact you. Watch the most common things as I've always told you; a fragrance, lights going on and off, things of that nature . . . that stuff happens, so just to be aware about it.

He said his one regret is that he never thought of the ramifications of his acts on other people. And he said, "For the first time in my life" and this is still his life, he says, "That's what's hitting me the hardest. The ramifications of what I do affects other people" and he said that he's feeling the intensity of other people feeling his loss and that's sort of like an echo flaps back on him, so his own act is now coming back to haunt him. He says, "Sometimes when I feel a little pulled down, I'm realizing it's not that I feel that myself" he said. Other people have felt frustrated about him. You know, they miss him or whatever. So he said, "Sometimes it's a little difficult" and that's what can send a person down. So that's why I always tell people, "Don't mourn a person when they go over, celebrate them and send them positive thoughts."

SHERI: So hard not to.

GLENN: Listen . . . I don't know. I've been doing this my whole life and I don't know if I could sit in that chair and go through what you are going through. I know a woman who was a bereavement counselor who lost her daughter and almost had to be put away. I can sit here and preach this all day but I don't know what I'd be capable of doing. I know in theory what's right but until you go through these experiences. He walked over to you again. He's got his hands on her shoulders. It's almost like she has to have something of his to hold on to. I feel like I'm holding someone's shirt or jacket. She may maintain something of his which he feels might help keep the link between the two of them. He will be around so you can talk to him or your dad. Your dad just stepped up. So just watch because you may have a few events where you might sense somebody around, so don't think you're crazy. In a way the move is going to be good because your father said the new environment will be such that it will be a new thing for you, a new start. It's very hard to be in an old place where you've been for so long and you look and you think, "Oh, my goodness, so and so always used to sit here."

So, once a day just talk to him for about two minutes a day. He will feel the intention. You can say something to him like, "Just let me know that you are okay" and then sit still for a moment. If you do it on a regular basis, he'll come through.

This session brought me enormous relief. Danny was okay, Danny was with my father, Danny had survived death, Danny was still Danny! I had believed that personality survives death for a long time, but when Danny passed, my sorrow was so great, that I was initially unable to access any of that knowledge. However, having this session changed everything by reassuring me of what I already knew: that Danny is still the same conscious being that I knew and loved, that he exists in a different dimension and that if I want to be in touch, I have to seek him where he dwells. The words came to me and I knew that I would spend a good portion of my time and energy exploring and learning how to connect-up with Danny.

One of the things that surprised me was the fact that Danny mentioned the "waves of prayer" that he experienced. I knew from my healing experience that energy directed to us here on earth from spirit could be very powerful because I've experienced it, but I didn't realize how powerful prayer could be when directed from us to spirit. It pleased me to think that those prayers reached him.

What I found very reassuring was the accuracy of everything Glenn talked about, right down to the last detail, from the fact that Dan had taken two different substances, to his reckless lifestyle, to his protectiveness of his younger sister. It was as if we were having a conversation, openly and honestly discussing what had taken place since the last time we had been together. Even more evidential to me was the fact that Danny was Danny. His personality was intact.

I believe that Dan's exposure to communicating through mediums prior to his passing meant that he would step up to the plate at every instance. Danny had had the opportunity to have two sessions with Glenn Dove in his own short life and my kids were used to hearing the "Mom Farewell Speech" if ever they left home, and it went like this: "Have a great time, take care of yourself and if anything happens, we meet at Glenn's." And so we did, one week after one of us left his home on earth for good. I can easily imagine my father saying to Dan, "Come on. I know the way to Glenn's from this end. I do it all the time to talk to your mother."

It began to occur to me that Danny and my father weren't hanging around the medium because they liked the medium but because they loved me. It was me they were staying close to and it was because they knew that I was going out to see Glenn that day that they made it their destination as well. As I left Glenn's office it occurred to me that Danny might just be leaving with me and that it would help me to think of him as being close to me. Since Dan obviously knew I was going to be at Glenn's that day it seemed to me that he couldn't be all that far away. From that time on it became easier for me to open the channels to "hearing" Danny and receiving messages and signs directly from him. Once I began to realize how close spirit must be to us, I began to pay more attention to what was going on inside my own heart and mind. As a result, I began to receive both thoughts and feelings that I felt, at the very least, were influenced by Dan.

CHAPTER THREE

Does Our Suffering Sadden Them?—
Words of Wisdom From Dan—
Dan Urges Us to Leave the Cemetery

We can't prevent ourselves from feeling enormous sadness when someone we love crosses over. It's built into the system and very little can be done. Anyone who has lost someone they love deeply understands the profound pain of mourning. It's like a chronic disease; you might experience better days, but it never completely goes away. Those of us who are bereaved, we know this to be true. Our loved ones are gone and we have been left behind to carry on. We have lost and we feel the hurt. It's agonizing and it's all about us. We seldom think about what those who have passed might be feeling. We somehow assume that they are over, and I don't mean in the sense of "over there" but in the sense of done, erased, finished!

Of course for me, by the time Dan passed, that was no longer my understanding of death, and that first session with Glenn Dove on July 8, 2008 fueled my confidence in Dan's existence and his continued love for us. From that time on it became easier for me to believe that Dan was close by and even possibly whispering in my ear. Not that I heard Dan's voice. It was my own voice that I heard, but when I was extremely sad and feeling guilty, it was the content of what I heard that made me sit up and think—for in the midst of despair came words of love and comfort. Even though it was hard to believe that these thoughts were coming from Danny, it was equally hard to imagine that I would supply that kind of balm to myself when I was so grief-stricken and guilt ridden.

On July 13, 2008, only twelve days after Danny passed, I was sitting on my bed (I spent a lot of time in bed), struggling again with those feelings of guilt, so prevalent in cases of death due to overdose and suicide. I was extremely upset when I began to hear what I thought were Dan's words in my head. I grabbed my computer and began to write what was coming into my mind. I call it: Words of Wisdom From Dan.

> You've got to develop a little bit more of that "fuck it" attitude. You can't sweat everything all the time. There is a medium ground between caring and not caring, the middle road, where you care, but not to the point of devastation. You will self-destruct. I, in life, leaned too far to the not caring side and therefore could not adequately protect myself. You, on the other hand, can sway so far to the caring side, that you do the harm to yourself without needing to put anything in your body. It comes right from the emotions into your physical body.
>
> I beg of you to lighten up, for your own sake as well as mine. Remember how you used to say that you are as happy as your most miserable child? Well, your misery can only bring me down because it fills me with remorse. I understand your dilemma, but understand mine. If you want to help me, to lift me up, then lift yourself up and you lift us both up. You are a strong woman mom, stronger than you think. Pool all your resources now that have gotten you through in the past. Know that I love you and always will

and that you are the one that always said, "Love is the only thing that spans the grave."

There will be time for us to venture forward and for me to join you in your work, as you have always known I would. Give me some time to get my bearings and I will come through for you time and time again. We will grow stronger and in time you will walk with both feet solidly on the ground, knowing that I am by your side at all times.

If you must cry mom, then cry for all those who are suffering now, they are all over the place—the lost and lonely ones, the poor and hungry ones, the sick and disabled ones, the oppressed and forsaken ones. Don't cry for me, for I am ok and so are you. This separation as you see it, is temporary and nothing so tragic has happened here. This is the life we lead, one that incorporates death as surely as it encapsulates birth and one cannot exist without the other.

Go forward in peace and trust that I am with you and that you have not been forsaken. You are only experiencing another facet of life that many have experienced before you and that many shall experience after you—the loss of a child. But those children are only lost to you in the flesh. In spirit each is alive and vital. If only you could see just a small glimpse more than you do. But remember, faith is belief in that which is not visible. If it were self-evident, why would there be any need for faith?

I leave you for now with the prayer that you rise up and live up to the knowledge that you have worked so hard to cultivate. I know that these are big words for me, but it is your vocabulary that makes this possible. I just send you the impression. You flesh it out in words.

Mom, I love you more than ever. Can you feel it? Open up your heart and feel it. It is stronger than the pain. Like

> you always said, Love is the strongest, most powerful force in the universe, the only thing that really makes life worth living, so feel it now.

I was moved by what I had written. I hadn't thought of my grief in terms of how it could be affecting Dan. I kept thinking about what he said about needing to lift myself in order to lift him.

> Well, your misery can only bring me down because it fills me with remorse. I understand your dilemma, but understand mine. If you want to help me, to lift me up, then lift yourself up and you lift us both up.

It made a lot of sense, especially in his case where he passed by his own hand. Knowing guilt all too well in my own life, I could easily understand feeling remorse if my actions had brought so much pain to so many. But how was I to lift myself? What a tall task, yet as his mother, how could I not try?

For the first time it really struck me that what I feel and do still affects Danny. This seemed radical to me, even though I had believed in the presence of spirit for a long time. Now I wondered how I could possibly think that Danny existed but was without any feelings. He may be a bloodless ghost but he is not soulless.

When I asked myself if there was any way that I could lift my spirits, I found myself confronted with enormous resistance to feeling better. There was almost an unspoken understanding that if Danny could not enjoy a good meal that I certainly shouldn't either. It seemed sacrilegious to do anything that my son couldn't do and even my breathing had become shallow.

However, now I felt obligated to think about Dan's words because they made sense. If I accepted that he had gone on (and I had), how could I negate his feelings? Wouldn't I feel remorse if my actions, accidental or otherwise, had brought about so much suffering to the people I loved?

As a mother, I have always tried to help my children in any way that I could, but this seemed an insurmountable task. Still, if it would help Danny, didn't I have to consider it? What I discovered was that I was not allowing myself to experience any happiness, because in light of Dan's passing, I felt it was wrong. I had a lot of thinking to do about this. If I was going to live believing in the valid presence of spirit then I had to make room for what it might be feeling. This wasn't only about me anymore but about Dan as well. By accepting his existence, I had to begin to listen to what he was saying and if my sorrow was causing him to feel remorse, then I knew I had to work on it.

> If you want to help me, to lift me up, then lift yourself up and you lift us both up.

I knew it wouldn't be easy . . . the joyous bereaved? Come on. Isn't that the biggest misnomer? But underneath all this confusion my heart was dancing to think that Danny still existed and that he was communicating his thoughts to me. I knew that I would continue to explore connecting-up with Danny in any way, shape, or form I could find. It brought me solace and sometimes, even joy. It seemed that Dan was urging me towards joy over sorrow, laughter over pain.

I vividly remember going to the cemetery sometime after Dan's funeral had passed. My husband and I stood at Dan's majestic gravestone and cried. We couldn't believe that this was where our son had ended up, under the ground at twenty-two years old, with nothing to mark his life but this black granite marker. I could see that Jerry was overwrought and then I heard these thoughts: "You guys can stand here and cry over this little piece of land all you want, but I'm not under there. I'm out here and I'm getting back in the car, and I'm riding shotgun." When I heard the words, "I'm riding shotgun" I woke up because "riding shotgun" was a big deal with Danny. The kids used to argue over whose turn it was to "ride shotgun" in the car. I strongly felt him urging us to remove ourselves from his grave because being there was unearthing raw emotions in both of us. Feeling this very strongly, I walked over to Jerry, took him by the arm and led him back to the car. "Danny wants us to leave," I said.

It was moments like this that made me believe that it was possible for me to have these communications with Dan at anytime and at any place. As time went on I began to benefit more and more from these moments of connecting-up. They filled me with a strong sense of Dan and helped me to miss him a little less. Admittedly, I can't see him and I'd give anything for five more minutes in his physical presence, but when I allow myself to feel him and to listen to his thoughts, I am to one degree or another, lifted up by them. Sometimes I cry, but it's a good cry.

CHAPTER FOUR

Loss, Guilt and An Astrological Reading

Guilt knows no boundaries. It knows no decency. It honors no situations. Guilt knows no logic. It attacks without warning and promotes an agonizing feeling that gnaws away inside of you.

In the face of loss, guilt can become a constant companion. It lingers in your mind, using every opportunity to remind you that you have failed. At a time when you need your own compassion mightily, you find instead an angry prosecutor in your mind, hurling accusations at you. "You should have done this! You shouldn't have done that!" You can't win.

One distressed mother wrote to me saying that she blames herself for her child's passing because she had been a proponent of "tough love" and hadn't listened to her child enough. A few months later an equally distressed mother contacted me expressing that she had not been tough enough with her child and had enabled his lifestyle, leading to his passing. Two completely opposite approaches resulted with the same outcome, and yet one thing rang clear to me regarding both of these mothers—and that was that they loved their children very much and acted out of love.

I have never been a stranger to guilt and in the situation of losing Dan, an angry prosecutor surfaced in my mind with plenty of ammunition to use against me. "You knew Danny was at risk," it would say. "Why weren't you more on top of it?"

I believe Danny passed at approximately 3:00 A.M. in the morning of July 1, in his sleep. Oddly, I awoke at 3:00 A.M. Going to the kitchen I found my daughter Jessica getting a glass of water and although it was summer and she didn't have school in the morning, I became extremely angry to discover her awake at that hour. It was an irrational anger, way over the top, and I even considered calling Danny to vent about Jessica because he and I enjoyed micro-managing her life together, but I reasoned that I was being silly and after a good hour of wrestling with my fierce emotions, I fell back to sleep.

Now, every time I thought back on it, I would get very angry at myself. I obviously knew something was going on, why didn't I do something? I kept kicking myself. How come I didn't act on that impulse to call Dan? I might have awakened him from his deathly slumber. It drove me crazy to think that I was awake at 3:00 A.M. that morning, that I experienced overwhelming emotions, that I obviously knew that something was wrong, but that I didn't know how to prevent it.

A few weeks later while unpacking boxes in the new apartment I came across a CD containing an astrological reading I had gotten in January of that year, a mere six months before Danny's passing. I had forgotten all about the reading and decided to listen to the CD. When I got to the section about Danny I was astounded to realize that I had literally been warned of the dangers that lie ahead. Why didn't I hear it this clearly back then? Why didn't I put that boy on a leash?

I decided to type up the information on the CD that was related to Dan. After reading and rereading it numerous times, it me how little I really know about the bigger picture. The owing excerpt from that session of January 8, 2008 with astrologer Robert Cook, helped me to see things from an expanded perspective.

Astrological Reading with Robert Cook—
January 8, 2008
Daniel Perl Migdol Born October 22, 1985

You're concerned about Daniel. His moon is in Aquarius and he's a Pisces rising. He has a very intense chart, this kid. He's a Pluto kid, which means he comes from some challenging beginnings . . . a bit of an angry fellow and between Pluto which smolders and the Uranus up at the top, he's a bit of a character, he's got a complicated nature about him. I am concerned about a couple of things here because he's born with so much Neptune, which is the substance abuse and he has a lax attitude and that's the Neptune. It's nice later in life to make adjustments, to make your life easier. Neptune has very little tolerance for dealing with discomforts so they always run to substances. They change how they feel but they don't really change anything about their lives. They move towards substances. They love to get high and their judgments tend to be terribly flawed. They just make bad decisions. And this Uranus up at the top makes him pretty much ungovernable because they have that attitude of "I'm going to do what I'm going to do" and that's it. They don't seem to have any remorse for anything they actually do, so there's a problematic attitude. They meet up with a few low life's along the way, so he's drawn to the underworld. It is very difficult to lead a legitimate life, if you will. Taking part in the world, that is very difficult to do and what I'm particularly concerned about over the next year is that Neptune is *really* going to be coming to town. Neptune's going to be sitting on top of his moon which for somebody else would be a very inspiring, creative beautiful moment.

For him it could be a time of major substance abuse. He has to be careful of becoming undone or doing something really stupid, a bad experience, or doing something that just really shoots himself in the foot. It's also possible because of the Neptune Moon, because the moon is like home, especially my family, especially my mother. She may be getting a little fed up with the whole thing and with the Neptune Moon, therefore he can end up feeling kicked out or cast adrift or cast out, because sometimes with Neptune Moon we lose our hope. We lose our roots. We lose our connection. A lot of people feel rootless with Neptune Moon. There may be some adjustment in the situation next year. He might just decide to take off and go who knows where. With Neptune Moon he could be a vagabond. It hasn't even begun. It's going to get very strong over the next year and you have to be very careful to stop him from coming apart. The best thing that could happen with the Neptune Moon would be that he meets some woman who helps put his life into order a little bit. It could be a good thing although I wouldn't count on it. But that would be a nice thing. It can also be a time when he can make some really horrible decisions, and really it's like come apart at the seams. And the other stuff is the twelfth house stuff where if you don't get your stuff together there is the possibility of incarceration. Whether you just feel imprisoned in your life, or imprisoned in your home, or literally you are in prison, it's like drifting, it's like you're just coming undone. He still has a ways to go, Sher. I still think the worst is probably still to come. This is a Neptune Moon aspect which is a terrible aspect of self undoing. Total fragility. It can affect his health, terrible judgments . . . well, we'll see. He's like a cat with nine lives, so he manages to survive this shit somehow, someway he does manage, but this is not an easy trip. That's Daniel. Good luck.

Up until I met Robert Cook, I thought of astrology as a fun game, but I never really considered it a serious science. However, in the light of this reading and a former reading with Robert Cook, my respect for astrology grew, along with my curiosity. In the first chart that Robert did for Danny approximately seven years prior, every one of Dan's issues was described with perfect accuracy. I was surprised to learn that information of this nature could be obtained by applying mathematical formulas to a specific date and time. It brought a change to my entire perspective when it dawned on me that Danny came into this life with all of those challenges already on his plate (or more accurately in his chart) and that those challenges had little or nothing at all to do with whether we were too soft or too hard as parents.

Whether you believe in the will of God, or chance, or something that falls in between the two, the important thing is to minimize your own self-importance in all of this. Certainly, as parents, we do our best to exert our influence, but our influence is one ingredient in a much bigger pie. I remember hanging up the phone after my first session with Robert Cook and thinking, "Maybe it isn't because I'm a soft mother that Danny has motivation issues."

For the first time it occurred to me that my guilt was actually based on conceit, or an overestimated sense of self. I took a giant step back and for the first time in my life I thought, "What kind of an ego must I have to think that because I love this child and want the best for him, that his life will go along in a certain way?"

When I realized this and admitted to myself how little I really knew about the bigger picture, I began to ease up a little on myself. Finally it seemed clear to me that I had to forgive myself for the fact that it wasn't in my hands to hold Danny here. After all, if it were in my hands to hold my child here, wouldn't I have done so? Wouldn't you have?

CHAPTER FIVE

Dan Gives Me My First Sign—
The Free Bird Incident

A week or so after Danny passed I was lying in bed, unable to bring myself to get up and get dressed. My heart was heavy and I could think of no way to lighten it. For lack of anything else to do, I opened my computer and began to look at the music that was listed in my iTunes library. My eyes immediately locked on a song by the name of "Free Bird." I had never listened to the song or had any interest in it before. It was included in a movie soundtrack that I had previously imported into my computer but now, for some unknown reason, I felt drawn to the song. As a matter of fact, I felt as if I had to hear the song. I hit play and proceeded to be astounded by the lyrics, because to me, the words could have been coming right out of Danny's mouth! Following are the lyrics to Free Bird:

> If I leave here tomorrow
> Would you still remember me?
> I must be traveling on
> Cause there's too many places I've yet to see
> But if I stay here with you now

Things just couldn't be the same
Cause I'm as free as a bird now
And this bird you cannot change
Whoa and this bird you cannot change
Lord knows I can't change
Lord knows I can't change

I sat in wonder. Could Dan possibly be sending me a message through this song? It certainly felt that way but of course, I couldn't know. The fact that I was drawn to listen to lyrics that touched me so profoundly, gave me cause to ponder. I decided to nickname Dan "Free Bird" for no other reason than it felt right. I knew that as a bereaved parent, my own imagination could be weaving the entire scenario to distract me from my pain. Every mother wants to believe that she is receiving messages from her child, however, six weeks later the plot thickened.

It was a warm, late afternoon in August when Jerry decided to play golf at the country club near our home in Ardsley that we had recently vacated. Feeling out of sorts and wanting to stay close to Jerry, I decided to accompany him to the club and ride around in the golf cart with him while he played. Now that we lived in the city, the golf course seemed very peaceful and serene, like a respite in the country. I have always found dusk an enchanting time of day, and so I accompanied my husband that day as he drove up to Westchester.

As soon as Jerry pulled off the highway, I was hit with a wave of sorrow. The familiar streets and stores where Dan and I had been together so many times were all around me and my heart began to ache. The pain literally felt like a knife in my chest, making me gasp for air. All I could think of was Danny and how much I missed him and how unbearable it was to accept the fact that he would never drive his car through these familiar streets again, or cook dinner for me in the Ardsley house kitchen. I began to regret that I had come up to Westchester in the first place. My heart, like a heavy weight was pulling me down into deep despair when I felt this huge, warm, presence surround me. Thoughts entered into my mind so quickly that I could hardly keep up with them. This is what I heard:

> Mom, stop idealizing me. It was not a bed of roses and it was never going to be. And whether you realize it or not, I am with you more now than I ever was then. Think about it, Mom. I didn't usually get up before three o'clock. When I did I could be very grouchy. Later in the day I would often go out with my friends and then stay up way late. Now I am with you all the time. Think of it this way . . . you used to worry about me all the time. Now you just miss me. That's not so bad. There are things worse than death, like incarceration Mom. Things were not going to be easy with me. I'm better now and that should make you feel better too. You don't have to be so sad. I'm okay, I still love you and I know that you still love me so feel better . . . please. When you are so sad, it makes me feel so guilty for screwing up. You have to try to feel better if you want to help me.

I was blown away because it all made sense and it sounded so much like my boy. It comforted me enormously and the pain in my chest began to ease. As we pulled into the parking lot of the country club, I blew my nose and wiped my face dry from the torrential flood of tears that soaked my cheeks. Jerry took off to the locker room while I began to make my way to the path that leads to the first tee, where I usually meet him. As I was walking along the tree-lined path, I spotted a group of men approaching me with their golf carts. Always the vain female my thoughts turned to all the crying that went on in the car. "Oh my God," I thought, "I must be a mess" and as I was fumbling in my purse for my pocket mirror I heard, "They are probably all assholes Mom, why do you care?"

Now, I can't even begin to tell you how much more that sounds like Danny than me. I started to laugh out loud and mentally I answered him back by saying, "Well Danny, they might not all be assholes but you're right, why do I care?" and I left the pocket mirror in my purse and met Jerry at the first tee, feeling very much better than I had in the car. Jerry played for a couple of hours as the sun set and the birds chirped and my heart felt a great deal lighter than it had in a long time.

However, as any bereaved person will tell you, the highs are short lived and as soon as we began driving back to the city, nagging doubts surfaced. "How do I know that was Danny speaking? It's probably just my imagination" and I persisted in this line of reasoning as we drove south on the Henry Hudson Parkway. I was beginning to lose heart when I got an idea. I would ask Danny to give me a sign. As we continued to drive south on the parkway with the Hudson River just to our right I mentally said, "Danny, if this is really you and not just my imagination, give me a sign." As soon as the words passed through my mind I had the impulse to look over at the river. To my astonishment, sitting right there, in plain view, was a beautiful white sailboat with the name FREE BIRD written across the side in big bold royal blue letters! "Oh my God" I thought, and I shouted out for Jerry to look quickly. Fortunately he caught a glimpse of the Free Bird before pulling the car off the highway. "Okay my boy," I said to Dan mentally, "You're on. From now on I will take you at your word and I won't doubt you ever!"

I can't say that I have always been able to live up to that kind of promise. Doubts do surface from time to time, but if what I hear in my mind sounds more like Dan than me, makes good sense and brings me comfort, I take it on faith that it is coming from him. After a sign like that, what would you do?

CHAPTER SIX

Our First "Purple Paper" Message with Roland Comtois—Aaron Finds the Watch and Coins

We were still in the process of packing up Danny's apartment, such a difficult thing to do. Making decisions as to what to keep, what to pass on, and what to throw away was almost impossible because these things were Danny's. You want to hold onto every thread for sentimental reasons, but we also felt that Danny would want us to give some of his things to the people he loved. So we did a good deal of giving away, as well.

We hadn't quite finished that job when I managed to arrange for a semi-private session with the medium Roland Comtois. I had seen Roland work numerous times in the past in large group sessions that were held at *Star Visions,* a spiritual center in Chappaqua N.Y. From the first time I sat in one of his group sessions I liked and trusted him. He was both gifted and compassionate. I was grateful that he agreed to meet with a smaller group. Aaron and Jessica joined me and on that day we met with Roland and three other people.

Interestingly, Roland receives messages for people months and even years in advance of actually meeting them. When these messages come to him he jots them down on big pieces of lilac construction paper, which he saves until he meets its recipient. Somehow he knows who the recipients are when he meets them and so he carries his papers around with him to all of his sessions in case the recipient is present. It's quite fascinating and Roland is currently working on a book called "The Purple Papers and the Stories Behind Them."

The session was very reassuring. Roland brought through the same familiar, loving, humorous messages that we were beginning to expect from Dan. We were still very hungry for continued reassurances that Danny was still Danny and so we were happy to hear much of the same things that we had already heard; that he regretted that we had not been able to say goodbye, that he slept through his passing and woke-up on the other side, and that my father had been there to help him.

I had only recently started to call him Free Bird, however at one point in the session I decided to try an experiment and so I literally sat there thinking, "Danny, say Free Bird—Danny say Free Bird," and a moment later Roland said, "He said to tell you that he is as free as a bird and that he has finally gotten his wings."

When we left *Star Visions* all three of us felt that Dan had definitely been present and had communicated with us through Roland. I was relieved because Roland was the second medium we were seeing since Danny passed and again, Danny was Danny. He kept making all of us laugh through our tears. We all treasured our "Purple Papers" which had individual messages from Dan for each of us, however, the one I want to talk about is Aaron's. On Aaron's Purple Paper there was a drawing of a watch as well as some coins, which Roland pointed out. He told Aaron that Dan wanted him to look out for a watch and some coins.

The next day when Aaron came into work he found a small box sitting on his desk. Two men who work for Jerry had finished packing up Dan's apartment and had brought over the last few boxes to our office, placing this small box on Aaron's desk. When

Aaron opened the box he found both Dan's watch and several coins. The coins he had given to Danny when he returned from a trip abroad and Danny had saved them. Apparently he wanted to be sure that Aaron got them back!

We were very touched by this and equally excited by the validity of the communication. It meant so much to us to know that Dan was still aware of things that are a part of our everyday life. Although he had passed, he was still interacting with us in the present. He was talking to us through Glenn and Roland and we couldn't get over how remarkable that was. We were still having a relationship with Dan and considering that he had passed, we thought that was pretty awesome!

CHAPTER SEVEN

Interesting Occurrences Continue to Happen—New Mediums—New Messages—New Signs

Summer 2008 was drawing to a close and Labor Day was approaching. The four of us, Jerry, Aaron, Jessica and I, made it through that first hellish summer, nursing deep, penetrating wounds. We pulled together like the cars of a wagon train would in order to keep insulated and connected. I was attempting to get us settled in our new apartment on West 99th street, and everything felt strange and unreal. So many things had changed so quickly. From suburban to urban, from house to high-rise, from driving to walking, from school bus to subway, each of us was learning how to live in this new environment that no longer contained Dan. Every now and then, one of us would spot someone on the street or in the subway that looked a lot like Danny and feel that heartbreak all over again. So we stayed a little closer to each other and we found comfort in that. Aaron began calling me more often to check on me and the four of us got together more frequently for dinner during the week. All of us had had at least one private session with Glenn Dove, three of us took part in the small group session with Roland, and each of us, in our own way, was feeling that Danny came around.

Sometimes Jerry and Aaron would go golfing up in Westchester and come back with stories of hawks and eagles that practically swooped down to touch their carts. Vivid images and strong feelings of Dan would often come to Jerry who began to see the golf course as a good place for him to experience Dan's presence.

Because Aaron had been foretold in a session with medium Glenn Dove that when Danny came around, he would play games with the electricity, he was not surprised when lights began to flash on and off in his presence. He could be walking down a busy street in Manhattan at night, stop at a street corner, and the light would blow out. And this could happen block after block.

I myself continued to feel Dan around. Although I never saw him or heard him audibly, there were moments when my memories would become so vivid and the feeling of love so overpowering that it felt as if his spirit was connecting-up with mine. Along with those strong feelings of love I was also comforted by what seemed to be Dan's words and his influence, coming into my mind.

Initially, I felt Dan's presence more often when I was sad, but as time went on I began to feel his presence in all kinds of situations. Sometimes if I am starting to get worked up about something I hear, "Mom, you are so dramatic," which always makes me step back and examine how I am looking at a given situation. I feel as if Dan keeps calling me out on things, but for my own good, so I don't mind.

I decided then, that the thing to do was to investigate the matter even further. I wanted to gather evidence that would prove conclusively that Danny existed. In my own mind I believed this to be true, but I wanted to make an in-depth exploration to accumulate more evidence for myself, as well as for others. Aaron offered to accompany me to any new mediums that interested me and so I began exploring different mediums, some in my local area and others at a distance. Sometimes we traveled, while at other times we remained at home and did telephone sessions. Investigating seemed to me like the most sensible thing to do, for I knew if I had lost Danny in this reality, I would surely be out looking for him. I would hire private investigators; I'd call out the National Guard! Wouldn't you?

My plan was threefold: I would continue to explore my own direct connection to Danny that came through my thoughts and feelings as well as dreams; I would explore connecting-up with Danny through reputable mediums; and I would continue to ask Dan for physical signs. I didn't want to burden Danny with a lot of demands but I was very intrigued by the Free Bird incident.

In the first two years I had medium sessions with at least fifteen different mediums. Some of those sessions were private, some of them were group sessions and occasionally I took part in a semi-private session, which consisted of six people to one medium, and I am happy to report that to this day, no matter where I go, Dan is Dan. He doesn't come through Glenn Dove one way and through Roland Comtois another. He is always humorous, he always makes the mediums laugh out loud and his story never changes. In keeping with what we know to be true, Daniel is always Daniel!

I've also received enough signs and messages directly from Danny to believe that anyone can connect-up. I am not a medium or a psychic. I am just a mother who misses her son and is willing to seek him through whatever means I find open to me. What I have discovered through my investigation is that connections between the physical and non-physical realms are indeed possible and beneficial to both sides. As I always say, don't take my word for it. Do your own investigating. That is the only way you will really know.

The Investigation Continues

CHAPTER EIGHT

Further Communications Continue Through "The Interstellar Telephone"—Danny Gets a Headstone—Danny Says "Thank You"

When I began delving into spiritualism in 1971, I couldn't have known that one day I would lose a beloved son at twenty-two years of age and need desperately to connect-up with him. However, when it did come to pass, this path to communication had already been paved for me. Fourteen years prior to Dan's passing I had pursued private sessions with Glenn Dove for the purpose of communicating with my father and Harry Edwards, on a regular basis. Glenn provided such a clear channel for me to my loved ones that I began to refer to this method of communication as "The Interstellar Telephone," like a reliable long distance phone call.

Naturally after Danny passed, trips to Glenn's office increased and at each session Dan would come through so like himself that I could easily recognize him. Through Glenn we talked about everything from family issues to events that were taking place in our lives at that time. If his gravestone was being completed, he knew it and would make a comment. If we did charitable work in his name, he knew it and expressed great pleasure. If I was disturbed about something he'd let me know that he was aware of my feelings and he would do his best to advise me, joking all the while that it was pretty funny to think of *him* giving *me* advice!

It became clear that in many significant ways, Dan was still part of our lives. He was intimately aware of everything that was going on with us and he was always confirming this through our encounters with mediums.

Sometimes Danny would simply comment on something that was happening in our lives that was connected to him. For example, when his gravestone was almost complete, in a session with Glenn Dove dated September 16, 2008, Dan made mention of it and said thank you.

> GLENN: Somebody just did something with his name or they're doing something with his name. His name was put someplace because he just said, "Thanks" and I ask him, "For what?" And he said, "They'll see" or "It's happening. " He sees it as if it's already happened. So, it's almost like when somebody's name is on something and it goes up . . . something with his name, an acknowledgement or recognition done for him.

That evening Jerry informed me that work on Dan's gravestone was underway and that it would be completed soon. I was happy to let him know that Danny had said much the same thing that day, as well as the fact that Danny had said thank you. I found it reassuring that Danny was aware of what was going on presently in our lives and that he was not stuck in the past. I know he's not here, but he can't be very far away because he knows everything and he has something to say about it. He even remembered to say "Thank you." What a guy!

CHAPTER NINE

Danny Puts Ideas Directly Into My Mind—Erin Receives a Christmas Gift From Danny—Confirmation on a "Purple Paper"

Usually when thoughts and ideas enter my mind that I feel are inspired by Dan, I think about them, but this was the first time the thoughts led me to take a physical action. It was December and I had purchased small holiday gifts for Aaron and Jess when one day, sitting around the apartment, the thought came to me that Danny wanted me to purchase a Christmas present for Aaron's girlfriend Erin, who he had known. The thought kept surfacing, "Mom, buy something for Erin from me." The thought persisted in my mind and so I responded to the thought. "Well, what did you have in mind?" I thought back as if talking to Dan directly, to which I heard, "Get her a pretty necklace from me, something with a heart on it." "That's easy enough," I thought and then I started to second-guess myself. Could this really be what Dan wants me to do? Should I trust this kind of thing? Am I losing it?"

Please understand, it's not as if I heard an audible ghostly voice calling out to me saying, "Sheeeeerrrrryyyyyyyy...... pleeeeaaaaaasssssseeeee gooooooo;" nothing of the kind. These thoughts enter my mind very quietly and at first glance, appear to be nothing more than my imagination. I'm sure you have these thoughts too. The difference is that I am paying attention to them, sorting through them and trying to understand their source.

I considered going downstairs and across Broadway to my favorite neighborhood jewelry store, *The Jewelry Boutique*. I knew I could find something there that Erin would love, but then I thought again, could this really be what Dan wants me to do? Should I trust this kind of feeling and respond to it?"

I analyzed the situation and reasoned my way through it. Maybe it was a message from Dan and maybe it wasn't, but following through, in a case like this, could only be a good thing. After all, purchasing a gift for my son's lovely girlfriend was something I should have done anyway. So I gathered my purse and headed to the store where I found exactly what I was looking for. I purchased a pretty gold heart on a delicate chain and waited while it was gift-wrapped beautifully. Happily, I headed home.

A week later I had the opportunity to be present in a group session with Roland Comtois, at *Star Visions* in Chappaqua, New York. Aaron and Erin accompanied me and unbeknownst to me, Erin was wearing the new necklace. About midway through the session Roland handed me one of his "Purple Papers" with a few messages written on it from Dan. The first one expressed his regrets that we had no time to say goodbye, which was true. The second simply said, "No more problems, no more problems," which brought me much relief. Underneath the written messages there was a drawing of a necklace with a heart on it. Roland then asked me what the necklace was about. I explained about the thoughts and feelings that led me to purchase the necklace and then Erin stood up and showed the group what she was wearing around her neck. Then to my amazement Roland said, Dan says, "Good job mom. You got it right!"

You can imagine my excitement to hear those words come out of Roland's mouth and to have the heart drawing on my purple paper; both confirmations of my experience with Dan. If it were not for these kinds of confirmations, however, I don't think I would have realized what was going on. It's way too easy to dismiss these thoughts as nonsense, especially when we are hard-wired to believe only what we see with our physical eyes and hear with our physical ears. But when the thoughts check out and you get that kind of verification, you can't help but step back and acknowledge that somehow we are communicating. Now I pay more attention to those thoughts because I know they come in intermixed with my own, but somehow communication is taking place.

CHAPTER TEN

Helping Ourselves By Helping Others—The Formation of The Daniel Migdol Memorial Fund—Danny Says "Keep It Going"

A few years prior to Danny's passing, Jerry and I had formed a small family foundation in order to give to others less fortunate than ourselves. We called it *The Migdol Family Foundation*, and although it is a small foundation, we found many ways to use the money to support families in the Harlem community, which is where Jerry maintains a real estate business. From school supplies in the fall, to camp programs in the summer, there is never any shortage of needs. We involve our own children as much as possible to show them the good that can be done when people care. Dan came to many of our events, helping to carry bags of toys and clothes that were being distributed. More often than not, the clothes, toys and school supplies were given out in backpacks or gym bags on which we would put our name and logo.

After Danny passed we decided to form *The Daniel Migdol Memorial Fund* so that we could distribute our gifts in his name. When the fall rolled around, instead of stopping our good will work, we decided to keep it going, only now, in Danny's name.

This gave us a new impetus and helped to keep us together in two very significant ways. We came to see that reaching out and helping others still lifted our hearts even though Danny had passed, and we derived satisfaction from seeing Dan's name on every backpack that was circulated. As Jerry said, "Dan didn't live long enough to make his own legacy, so we will make one for him."

That fall brought the usual call for school supplies in September and turkeys at Thanksgiving. When Christmas time rolled around, everything from warm mittens to stuffed animals were requested. We did our best to come up with a quality assortment of age appropriate gifts and packed them into Daniel Migdol Memorial Fund bags, including a small written note from Jerry, explaining who Danny was and what he means to us.

We felt really good about this. I hoped that Danny was aware of it and that it pleased him too. Intrinsically, I thought that it must. Then in March of 2009 Jerry joined Aaron, Erin and me for a trip back to *Star Visions* in Chappaqua, New York where Roland was holding one of his group sessions.

Following are the words that were spoken to Jerry from Dan through Roland Comtois in March of 2009.

ROLAND: You feel your boy? Right here, right now, in this moment, his hands on your shoulders? He's standing there with all of his strength, he's not a lost soul. I have to tell you Jerry, he's just not a lost soul, not on any level, not anywhere inside. He said he had gone through a lot of his own things in here, (points to heart and head) in here, you know? And he put you on a roller coaster ride and he's so sorry that he did that to you, he says. He's so sorry that he made you go up and down, and up and down. "I'm sorry I drove you guys crazy," he says. "I'm sorry that I drove you guys crazy." He says he wants me to thank you for the memorial, "The MEMORIAL" he says, "All the things you're doing in MY NAME!" He says "Thanks for working that out for me." You know how he gets, he's like...

> Wow, me... yeah... yeah, like this... he says, he wants you to know that he's so grateful for that. He's so grateful for that and he wants you to know to keep it going. He says, you can do it, He says, "I know mom tires you out a little bit, but keep it going!"

We sat there laughing our heads off. Unfortunately the written word cannot convey the humorous way that Roland strutted around the room impersonating Danny boasting and bragging about his name. Again, I was overjoyed to receive confirmation that Danny knew about The Daniel Migdol Memorial Fund and that he was grateful for it. His reaction clearly demonstrated to me that our loved ones don't want to be forgotten just because they have passed to the other side. On the contrary, they want to be remembered, and they want to be talked about, laughed about, toasted to.

And keep in mind that you don't need a lot of money to do something wonderful in your loved one's name. One of the bereaved fathers I know organizes a toy collection in honor of his son who spent his last Christmas in the hospital. Every Christmas he delivers these toys to children spending their holidays in the hospital. It brings joy to every child who receives this unexpected gift, and I know it brings a wonderful feeling to both my friend and his son on the other side. I also know a bereaved mother who collects used coats and sews labels in each coat that contain her daughter's name. She distributes the coats through her church at Christmas time. I'm sure it brings her some solace and others a needed winter coat, but when you add to that equation that her daughter on the other side feels honored too, as Dan would say, "It's all good!"

These small things that we can do to help others, carry us over some of the rough spots, especially around the holidays. At the same time, I love that we are honoring Dan. He says for us to "Keep it going" and I'm sure we will, Danny boy!

CHAPTER ELEVEN

Aaron's Experience with Dan and the Lights—A Confirmation at Our First Blindfold Billet Reading with Rev. Dr. Ron Fredrics—Dan Gets His Way

As mentioned earlier, shortly after Danny passed, Aaron began to have experiences with lights going off and on in his presence. Happening with both streetlights in rural and urban areas, house lights in his apartment and the apartments of others, wherever Aaron went these occurrences took place. I was with him on a number of occasions when this happened and there is no question that lights just randomly went out. I saw a video Aaron had made one night while visiting our old neighborhood in Hastings-on-Hudson, New York. In a quiet cul-de-sac after sunset Aaron was filming a streetlamp light as it went out. Five seconds later he recorded his voice as he said, "Turn it back on Dan," and to my amazement, within another second it came back on again.

One morning Aaron reported waking from his sleep at approximately 3:00 A.M. and going to the window of his apartment that overlooked a vacant building under construction. There was no one living in the building and no one on the premises at that hour, however, Aaron witnessed an incredible light show as each floor of the building took its turn in lighting up. He just stood there and watched it, amazed and amused. He was quite certain that the light show had been a little entertainment from Dan. More evidence to Aaron of Dan's horsing around is how frequently his television goes on and off while he is busy working in the next room. These electrical occurrences kept on throughout the remainder of 2008 and continued into 2009. Then in the spring of 2009 there was an interesting development.

I had never heard of "Blindfold Billet Readings" before. I had no idea what to expect on this night of May 15, 2009 when I went with Aaron and Jessica to a church in Greenwich Village where a spirit communicator named Reverend Dr. Ron Fredrics was doing Blindfold Billet Readings. Ron had been highly recommended to me by my dear friend Reverend Dr. Joyce Liechenstein , who had seen Ron's work before and had made it very clear that this was one medium I would not want to miss.

When we arrived at the church it was already filling up. By the time Ron arrived the room contained 125 people, all excited and talking amongst themselves. As Ron walked up to the front of the room to take his place behind his podium, I was impressed with his well-groomed and dashing appearance. As he spoke briefly about his work and future projects, little pieces of white lined paper were circulated to everyone in the room along with pens. Ron then explained that the pieces of paper were billets and went on to give us very explicit instructions as to how to fill them out. He told us that we could write the names of three people in spirit who we would like to contact and to indicate what their relationship was to us. We were then told that we could write one question and below the question we were to print our names. Each of us then folded our billets in half and they were collected in a basket that was attached to Ron's podium. Naturally I assumed that the medium would open up each billet and read it, attempting to connect-up with those particular people written on the paper. How wrong I was.

Ron asked the group to help him enter into a trance by singing a few verses of "Cum Baya." Of course my kids balked, however I assured them that it was a good way to invite in the spirits. Then, to my amazement, while the singing ensued, Ron taped both of his eyelids shut and then fastened a blindfold over that, adjusting it so that he could not see. At some point during that brief time he must have slipped into trance, because a moment later he reached for the first billet which he felt between his fingers, and then held up to his forehead or the back of his head. A moment later he started to speak and then I was really impressed. With an eloquence and articulation as I have never heard before with any medium, Ron began pronouncing lengthy first and last names. Never did he call out a name that wasn't recognized and spoken for. He answered every one of one hundred and twenty-five billet questions with stunning accuracy, for I observed the reactions of the others in the room and they were both stunned and moved to tears.

However, nothing could have prepared me for what happened with us. Before I go into it, I'd like to show you what Aaron's billet looked like. As you will see, he had his brother's name on top, my father's name second, and my grandfather he listed third. His question had to do with the lights and then he wrote his name:

Daniel Migdol—brother
Herman Perl—grandfather
John Oxfeld—great grandfather

When the lights go on and off are you doing it?

Aaron Migdol

After Ron had done approximately twenty-five readings our ears perked up when we heard the following:

RON: I have an Aaron here, Migdol.

AARON: Yes, that's me.

RON: He came very quickly. He came very quickly. Of course, Danny was speaking to you.

AARON: Yeah.

RON: And Herman is speaking to you. They're saying, "When the lights go on and off, we're doing it. We want you to know we're there."

AARON: That's amazing.

RON: They want you to know they're there. Someone is walking around saying, "I have nothing to do with this." His name is John, "I had nothing to do with this," he says, but a brother and a grandfather definitely had a lot to do with it.

AARON: That's incredible!

I could only agree with Aaron on that one. It was incredible and it certainly validated the incidents with the lights, and Danny's continued existence in spirit, but that was not all Dan had in store for us that night.

I've come to see that one of the many benefits of billet readings is that everyone who fills out a billet is guaranteed a reading. That's not usual in big group sessions where most of the time, the name of the game is "Which spirit shouts the loudest." It's almost like a free-for-all and I've had mediums tell me that many spirits were shouting in their ears all at once, and that before they could complete one reading they were moving on to another. However, with billets that's never the case. I'm reminded of the old Jewish Deli method of: take a ticket, wait your turn. It certainly makes group sessions much less chaotic, for the medium as well as the spirits, who seem to understand the routine and wait their turn. The medium reads for each person who has filled out a billet. When he finishes a reading he takes another billet and moves on to the next reading. I think this is what Ron had in mind because after he completed Aaron's reading, he reached into his basket for the next billet to read. Danny, however, didn't want to let him move away from us just yet. I watched for a moment as Ron paused and refrained from taking another billet and then he continued speaking:

RON: He says, it's not only that I have a lot to do with it, but I think that I have a sister in the room. Is there a sister nearby somewhere?

JESSICA: (quietly) Yeah. (Jessica put only Dan's name on her billet and asked him if he can hear her when she talks to him.)

RON: Is there a sister here by the name of Jessica?

JESSICA: (very quietly) Yeah.

RON: He's talking to you. I have the sound of Daniel again. "When you talk to me" he says, "talk like that. When you talk in public, boom! I hear you and if you quiet your mind, breathe in deep, hold your breath you will hear me tell you the answers. Go for the white light all around you."

Now as before, Ron finished the reading and attempted to move on, away from Danny and to the next billet but again Danny must have tried to hold him back because this is what we heard next.

RON: Come on, cut this out. What are you kidding me? What are you kidding? Daniel stop this, you're throwing one after another at me!"

Then Ron paused for approximately ten seconds and said:

RON: Oh, bless you. Not only is Daniel here, but Perl...

SHERI: Yes.

RON: I believe he's not a brother, but he is your son?

SHERI: Yes.

RON: Talk to me. Talk to me... Herman, Herman, I believe he may be a father?

SHERI: He's my father.

RON: Is it spelled differently? but in front of me I have something that looks like a pearl and that's also the name of your guide and I believe that you understand what the word pearl means... I think Perl is your maiden name.

SHERI: Yes it is my maiden name.

RON: We are doing everything around you Sheri, to take that body into fulfillment, to give you healing, life and love and know that the spirit world is with you one hundred percent of the time to keep you well, to keep your children well.

SHERI: Thank you.

I had put Danny, my father Herman Perl and Harry Edwards, my spiritual healer, on my billet. In my question I had asked if the spirits are really around me when I do my healing work and the answer was that they are one hundred percent of the time. I was overwhelmingly happy with the messages that had come through for they were just what I needed to hear. I walked out of the church feeling very pleased, for my investigation was yielding more and more evidence that Danny remained close to us and that he had certainly gotten proficient at playing with the electricity!

CHAPTER TWELVE

Prayer Helps Everyone—The Forming of the Prayer Registry—Dan's Involvement with the Prayer Registry

Every year now, as the warm spring weather begins to yield to the hotter days of summer, I am filled with memories of Dan's last days. Haunting feelings of loss and sadness trickle through the heat and threaten to wash me away into a state of longing for something that was once taken for granted. I try to remind myself that the lesson is to take nothing that I love for granted; not my loved ones, not my health, not the roof over my head. I wonder why it is so easy for me to lament so much about Danny and still take Aaron, Jess and Jerry for granted all the time. Is it inherent in the nature of human beings to only know what they've got when it's gone?

As the first anniversary of Dan's passing was approaching, heralded by the summer heat that seemed to be swallowing up my air, I knew that we needed some kind of support to help us get through the dreaded day of July 1, 2009. We didn't want to ask our family or friends to interrupt their work schedules to be by our side, yet we felt the need to do something.

When Jerry suggested that we simply ask everyone to send out a prayer, the idea smacked of rightness. No one would have to take off from work, no one would have to travel, and no one would be put out. "That's easy" I thought, and went about setting up a prayer team by sending out emails and making phone calls. By the morning of July 1, we had assembled quite an army of prayer givers and they must have started praying very early that morning, because I woke up with less angst and sorrow than I ever thought possible. It was impressive to all four of us, for we all felt stronger and better for the prayers. As the day drew to a close, I began to think about how much the prayers actually helped us and what a wonderful thing it would be to open this up to others in the same way.

More than once since he made the crossing Danny had come through to say that those prayers sent to him when he passed had helped him to heal. It was clear to me that the prayers had helped us. It occurred to me then that I would have to find a way to set up a prayer team and organize a system for sending prayers to children on the other side, as well as their families here on earth on their passing dates.

The moment I had the idea, I felt wonderful about it. I knew instinctively that others would surely benefit, but how to go about it and how to set it up was an enigma to me. Fortunately, my son Aaron showed up one day and set up the entire website. The children's names would be printed onto their passing dates on The Prayer Registry Calendars and once inputted, the names would remain on their dates year after year. The Prayer Registry sends out one-day reminders before each child's Prayer Date to the entire Prayer Team, however, the Google calendars are public so anyone can check my website www.sheriperl.com to see who is due for prayer. The Prayer Team is made up of all the parents who have registered their children and they are a strong and beautiful band of parents who are dedicated and committed to the cause of praying for each and every child who is registered, and their families as well.

Each member of The Prayer Team prays in their own corner of the world, in whatever way is natural to them. The Prayer Registry is an interfaith organization. All faiths and beliefs are welcome and all people are respected. We are mothers and fathers from all over the globe who have lost one or more children. Our religions and backgrounds vary, but our intention is the same: To send loving, healing energy to the spirits of our beloved children and their families. Each of the children and their families are the focus of this mass prayer every year on the Prayer Date of the child. Sometimes we have four children being held-in-prayer on the same date, so we send out our thoughts to all of them and to all of their families as well. When I think about it, it's the least we can do and the most we can do at the same time, for it takes only a moment to send a prayer, but it actually penetrates the veil and lifts up our loved ones! To know that there is actually something positive that we can still do for our children who have passed, affords us parents a little bit of solace.

I received an even greater gift when I learned of Danny's interest and involvement with The Prayer Registry. The following information came through in a session that Aaron had with medium Glenn Dove:

September 11, 2010: Glenn Dove with Aaron—Dan and Herman present

GLENN: Dan says not necessarily by choice but by circumstance he's become the other side counterpart for the work that your mom's doing here. He said it's almost like she's entertaining the network on this side. She's setting it up and she's putting this out and as a result he's receiving these energies and these feelings from people. So what's happened is, Dan, by process of association, does the spirit side of your mother's work. She's doing this side, and he's working on that side of the curtain. She's in one room, he's in the other room, and they're both doing the same thing.

AARON: Oh, that's great!

GLENN: And he starts to laugh cause he goes, "I didn't have much choice" because it's almost as if families and people that she's affecting who in turn send him thoughts, he's meeting their families. It's kind of been like a looping network. He says, "I don't know how I wound up like this but it just worked out that way." So, I can't say it was something he did by choice but he makes a joke, "It's something that I fell into." So it's almost like you work with your father, he works with his mother. That's exactly what it is.

AARON: Well, she has this Prayer Registry.

GLENN: Well it's that and it's all her other work. He says, "They're going to ask what I'm doing. It isn't like a job, it isn't like I'm an attorney or I'm an accountant over here, because obviously we don't have those things." He said that he's running the spiritual side of The Prayer Registry, well he's trying to. Your mother's running the material side, the world side, the earthly side and he's connected with it over there.

He said that, and your grandfather chimes in as well: "Your mother's always wanted to make a change. She's always had this, in a good sense, hippy kind of mindset. She came in; she's one of these people who would be against war and stuff like that. Her work on this side from the get-go was to be healing and service. Dan says, "I'm only glad I can be part of it." He goes, "I can't take as much credit as her because she's a tireless worker" and she doesn't see, most people don't, but especially for her, because she's so wrapped up in doing things and talking and helping, she doesn't see how much effect that she's having. Dan just sometimes feels funny because it's his name and it's him that was the trigger, the spark that ignited the fire. So sometimes, he goes, "It seems like it comes back to me but," he says, "I can't seriously even think about it, I'm like the least." But he's trying and that's what he's doing now but the cause of it . . . he did something off the wall stupid, it's like he kicked over the bucket by mistake and it starts the fire and burned down a bad building or something like that, so people are cheering. So through an error on his part, it snowballed into a positive situation but then it kept going and he goes "And it came back and hit me" and so by a mistake on his part he puts himself over and starts the chain reaction. It's like that game mousetrap where you hit the ball and it rolls down and flips the thing, all of a sudden. He says "But now it's coming full circle" and by him witnessing all of it, it's now got him involved in it. So, I said it before. It works out perfectly. He works for your mom. You work for your dad.

Dan says, "So many people come over here who deserve what I have and don't get it. So many people come over and have done right on your side and don't get what I have." He says, "Sometimes I feel a little weird because" he says, "It happened to me on both sides. I was on this side and got quite a lot given to me." I guess he means his needs were met, in the outer sense. He lived with a good family; he always had a roof over his head. He was always provided for. Dan says, "So many people don't even have that on the earth. I kind of had it and then I come over here and what happens? The same thing. This is my life. I can't escape it. And he says that's when he had to go with it. He tried to escape it by going over, escape the fact that he was given everything in the outer sense and in the loving sense and fucked it up in plain English. And he says, I get over here and what happens? In the spirit sense I'm gonna

> get everything. It's almost like "What did I do to deserve this?" So he says, "Bing, the light finally went off... well then Dan, I'm going to earn it. I have to now work for what I've already been given." Some people work and then they get something, Dan's on the opposite track. He's going to have to now work for what he's already been given because he says, "I'm not doing it because anyone is making me. I'm doing it because for the first time in my life, I feel it!"
>
> Now this comes full circle. He's telling me that it's the group here holding him up. It's almost like, you look down and everyone down here has their hands up and it's like he's standing on them, holding him up.

When I heard this on the recording I was thrilled. What a beautiful image for what we do at The Prayer Registry! We are lifting them up with the energy from our prayers. As parents, there is some tangible relief from knowing that we can still affect our children's lives in a positive way.

On May 21, 2011, I was honored to host an evening of Blindfold Billet Readings with spirit communicator Ron Fredrics in my home in *New York City*. You have read about Ron in a former chapter. He is the medium who answered Aaron's question regarding the lights going on and off back in May of 2009. Now, on this occasion I decided to use my billet to ask a question about The Prayer Registry. I addressed my question to Danny and I asked him if he could tell me about how the prayers come to them. This was the answer I received:

> **RON:** Danny comes in very strong and he's saying "These words you are using and the group is using, don't just go into the ether, they go into the ether and rise up and they create a beautiful color, beautiful aura around all those

> who truly need it. Your work is commendable they are saying: Commendable."

In my opinion what is commendable is the devotion of all the parents who comprise The Prayer Team. It has become a way of life to pray for these children and their families who go on living despite their losses and in return, we are all enriched by the prayers of love that we send out. When our own child's dreaded Prayer Date arrives, we feel stronger for the prayers that are being directed to us, and we take heart in knowing that so many people are praying for our child. It's just a small measure of solace, however, in this arena of loss and bereavement, we'll take whatever solace we can get.

There is no fee to register a child with The Prayer Registry and everyone is welcome. Simply email me at: theprayerregistry@gmail.com and tell me the full name and passing date of your child and it's a done deal. Your child and your family will not have to face another Prayer Date without the support of many. On behalf of myself, and the rest of The Prayer Team, I extend a warm invitation.

CHAPTER THIRTEEN

There's No Doubt About It, Dan Sees, Feels and Hears Me—I Throw a Hissy Fit, Danny Calls Me On It—An Amazing Experience in Rhode Island

On December 11, 2010 I took part in an all day conference that was held in Warwick, Rhode Island. It was organized and hosted by the profoundly gifted medium Roland Comtois. I have enormous respect for Roland, so when he invited me to take part in his conference, I was honored. The one-day event, referred to as "The After Loss Campaign" had approximately sixty volunteer contributors. I had my own table where I was able to represent The Prayer Registry and sign up children for prayer. I spent most of the day at my table, talking about the registry and passing out my new Prayer Registry cards. I left my table, however, for the two events in which Roland was channeling messages.

The first session met between 11:00 A.M. and noon. There were approximately three hundred people present, and of course everyone wanted to receive a message from a loved one. As I always say, the name of the game in large group sessions is which spirit shouts the loudest, and I knew that there were people present who needed a message far more than I did. Aside from the fact that I go to more mediums than anyone I know, and that I had recently been in a smaller group session with Roland and received quite a long message from Dan, there were people present who were suffering greatly from very recent losses and had not yet been connected-up at all. One father who had recently lost his son was so broken up, all I could do was pray that his son would come through, and he did!

Ordinarily I am pretty greedy in these situations, but I steered myself towards being gracious and generous, telling myself to be happy for those who received messages and for the opportunity to witness the communications taking place. I'll admit I was a little antsy at times, but for the most part I was a "lady" about it and felt genuine joy for those who were connected-up.

Later that day Roland held one final session between 4:00 P.M. and 5:00 P.M. The group was much smaller this time, with approximately thirty people present. Again I told myself to make no demands and to be happy for others who were receiving messages. I managed to keep it together for the first thirty minutes and then all hell broke loose!

I won't try to hide the fact that deep inside myself, a woman of sixty years, there is also a little girl who can raise quite a ruckus. Of course, the woman of sixty years wasn't about to throw a hissy fit in that room but the little girl had no problem throwing a hissy fit inside my head! As if little Sheri was just standing there stamping her metaphysical foot, these are the thoughts that were running through my head:

> God damn it Danny, where the hell are you? Do you mean to tell me that I'm not even going to get one word out of you? That isn't fair. I'm happy to be here for others but what about me????? You know, I came a long distance to be here too. Listen Danny, I really think you should be coming through.

I went on and on like that nonstop. I was relentless and I was emotional. Then, all of a sudden Roland looked me in the eye and said:

ROLAND: Your boy is here, Sheri.

SHERI: Good.

ROLAND: Your boy is here, Sheri. He says, "What do you think?" He says, "I'm just here, present, to be with you. That's it. Let's not make it a big deal anymore," he says.

SHERI: That will be the day.

ROLAND: He did say you get a little dramatic though, in your noisy mind! He says just be present for him.

That was it, but that was enough. Dan had put me in my place! The session ended shortly and when I returned to my hotel room I had a good laugh. My behavior had been so childish and truth be told, I was able to hide it from everyone in the room with the exception of Danny who could see everything. I wondered, who else in spirit was watching me throw this hissy fit and if this meant that I would finally have to grow up!

The best part of this event for me, however, was the reassurance that not only is Danny around, but he is acutely aware of my feelings. He called me out on my "noisy mind" which is so like Dan. This also illustrates to me that although Danny and I are in separate realities right now, those realities can't be very far apart because Dan was totally aware of what was going on inside my mind. It occurred to me that the spirit world could be right here within this very world we are in, and that what separates us could best be described as different vibrational frequencies rather than actual distance. I can't see Dan and I can't hear Dan's voice, but I do hear thoughts in my head that I feel are coming from him and if I've heard this once, I've heard it a hundred times, "Mom, you are so dramatic." So, time goes on and so does this relationship between Danny and me and as much as I'd trade my right arm to have him here in the flesh, I'm so grateful to be able to still communicate with him in spirit.

I don't think the day will ever come when I have no need for reassurance, but I do know that over time my trust deepens. Maybe one day I can "just be present" for Danny as he requested without demanding endless proof that he is himself and that he is still with me. But I am getting to believe it more and more which is why I am passing this knowledge on to you, that you may know it too.

Our children are as close as our breath and our relationships continue through all time. Send them your love. They can feel it. Breathe in their love. It is all around you. Danny says so!

CHAPTER FOURTEEN

Creating Sacred Places—Dan Comments on His Crowded Altar—Dan Tells Jerry to Head East to Central Park*—Danny's Bench*

One of the things that you can do for yourself is to designate a certain place, in or around your home that can be dedicated to your loved one. I set up one in my apartment that I call Danny's Altar, however if the religious connotation of the word altar bothers you, it could just as easily be called Danny's Place or Danny's Corner. None of that matters, because whatever you call it, once you set it up, it becomes sacred. It becomes sacred ground because you dedicate it to your loved one and place on it some of the personal items related to your loved one that have meaning for you.

Once we were settled, one of the first things that I did in the apartment was set up Danny's Altar. I wanted one specific place where I could lay out some of Danny's personal things, such as his wallet and the little book that contains two poems he had written. I had a piece of furniture in the living room, a chest of drawers with a nice tabletop about waist length high, so I took everything off the tabletop and went about decorating it with numerous photographs of Danny, candles, the paw print of our dog Genevieve and Danny's small urn containing her ashes. It's also crowded with many little gifts that Danny bought for me on his trip abroad with his friends, taken a few months prior to his passing. Everything on the altar has something to do with Danny. When one of us finds another item of Dan's, it gets placed on the altar. It's gotten very crowded.

I like to light the candles that are on the altar and to keep Dan's face prominent in our home. We may have to live without his physical presence, but we don't have to box his things away and try to forget. I'm not even capable of doing that and I know it's the last thing that Danny wants. To me, this sacred corner creates a space where it feels safe to look at Danny's things. I think it is when you are caught off guard and don't expect to see something, that a glimpse of a wallet sitting in a drawer for example, can erupt your raw emotions. So, as things of Danny's turn up, they all make their way to his little shrine and I love it. When people come to visit, they don't have to be afraid to mention his name. It brings the "elephant in the room" right out into the open and if others are uptight to mention his name, I'm certainly not!

In a session with medium Roland Comtois on March 4, 2010, Danny let me know that he is well aware of the altar's presence and in his own inimitable way, he teased me about it.

> ROLAND: Dan says he loves the altar or something. Some place where all his things are. He says, "My God, can it get any bigger?" He says, "If it gets any bigger then it is now, you'll need another room. It's okay, it's not bad," he says. "But there's a few more things you could put there" he says. God, he's a riot.

You can always rely on Dan to find the humor in everything.

Some people plant memorial gardens while others get memorial tattoos. It doesn't matter what you do or how much or little

Above is a photograph of the crowded little altar that you've just read about.

it costs. What does matter is that you have a sacred place somewhere in your home, around your home, or on your person to remind you of your loved one, without catching you off guard.

I do believe that our loved ones on the other side appreciate these gestures and that they become focal points that help draw them a little closer to us. Danny never misses an opportunity to let us know that he is aware of and interested in all of the things that we have dedicated to him. In group sessions I have heard many spirits express knowledge of and gratitude for tattoos dedicated to them.

Sometime after Danny passed Aaron was walking in *Central Park* when he noticed that many of the benches had memorial plaques on them honoring people who had passed. He thought they were awesome and immediately thought of purchasing one for Dan. He spoke to Jerry about it and they both agreed that it would be a good thing for us. We lived only a few blocks west of *Central Park* and we could visit the bench all the time.

Jerry and Aaron found a bench for Dan in a dreamlike section of *Central Park* with a beautiful lake, several waterfalls, huge trees, lots of animals and many, many birds including ducks on the lake. It's hard to believe that this setting is located in the middle of *New York City*. This little paradise is surely the perfect place for a bench for Dan who used to refer to the city as "The Concrete Jungle."

I like to visit the bench. It gives me a reason to get out and walk and once I get there, I am touched by the sheer beauty of nature. It is Jerry, however, who really feels close to Dan on the golf course and in the park.

In May of 2011, we were hosting spirit communicator Ron Fredrics in our home for an evening of his Blindfold Billet Readings. Before going into trance, Ron said that he had a message for his hosts and proceeded to tell us this:

> **RON:** This is a very odd thing I'm picking up for the two of you, especially Jerry. He says to me, "If you want to really feel" I know we're way on the west side but I'm taking you to the east side. And he says "You need to feel my presence

and to communicate in *Central Park*." Does that make any sense to you?

JERRY: Yes.

RON: It does? You know something about *Central Park*?

JERRY: I know a lot about *Central Park*. That's where his bench is.

RON: His what?

JERRY: His bench. I have a memorial bench for him.

RON: There you go! He says, "Come to me at *Central Park*." It gets me teary-eyed.

It pleases me to know that Danny is cognizant of all the things we are doing. It doesn't bring him back but it demonstrates that communication is possible, despite the separation. It's pretty obvious that everything we do for Danny pleases him and that he brings his consciousness to those places and appreciates all the love that went into them. It pleases me to realize that anything we do for ourselves in their names is a gift to them, as well.

A sacred space can be created with as little as a photograph and a candle. However great, however small, these sacred spaces lift us up, those of us on both sides.

Sheri at Dan's bench in the summer of 2010. The plaque reads:

IN LOVING MEMORY AND TRIBUTE
DANIEL PERL MIGDOL
ENJOY DAN'S SPECIAL PLACE
SHERI JERRY AARON JESSICA

CHAPTER FIFTEEN

Asking Dan for More Signs—Finding Signs on a Book Cover and at The Apple Store, Documented with Photographs

There is no question in my mind that if you go to a good medium you can get connected-up, but for many people it is simply not affordable. I do believe, however, that each of us can make these connections on our own and one of the ways to do that is through using signs.

I don't have a clue how the spirits can make some of this stuff come about, but I know they are playing a part. In the next two stories, I simply asked Dan for signs and they were instantly supplied, making it appear that they (the signs) were actually in place before I had the impulse to ask for them. The first one had to do with a book that was sitting on my lap.

One of my favorite books concerning conditions on the other side is titled, "Testimonies of Light." It is written by British medium Helen Greaves, whose other book, "The Wheel of Eternity," had just arrived in the mail from Amazon. It was a small paperback book, which I took out of the package and placed on my lap as I sat down at my computer to finish writing the Free Bird Chapter. I was reading over the Free Bird chapter when I thought, "Gee, that was a really good story Dan and an even better sign, but I haven't had another sign since Free Bird, and that was almost a year ago! Don't you think it's about time I had another?" To my surprise I heard these words come into my mind, "Well, mom, just take a look at the book on your lap."

"The book on my lap? Okay" I thought. I picked up the book and I turned it around and around and then my eyes settled on the word and symbol that were imprinted on the binder. First I saw the name Daniel and just above the name there was a bird

This is the photo of what I saw on the side of the book.

with it's wings stretched up as if about to take off in flight. "Oh My God" I thought, and grabbed my handy little iPhone camera. I mean, what are the chances???

Another story about an instantaneous sign, and by that I mean one that showed up a mere second after it was requested, happened in *The Apple Store*.

I needed some help with a computer problem, so I scheduled an appointment at *The Apple Store*. The store is always crowded, so the procedure is to check in with one of the staff members and then to wait and watch for your name to show up on one of the large blue screens mounted on the wall. When your name moves into position one, you are next in line for an appointment. I checked in as Sheri Migdol as that is my married name. I was told to find a seat, that they were running a little bit late, and to check the screens for my name to come up.

A few minutes later I found an empty chair and no sooner had I sat down than I had the impulse to ask Danny for a sign. It was merely a fleeting thought, however, I acted on it. I mentally said, "Okay Danny, give me a sign." A second later I had the impulse to look for my name on the blue screen and what I saw was pretty surprising. There were twelve names listed on the screen. Next to number 7 it said, sheri m. Just above that, number 6 read, "Daniel M." Now I ask you, with all the possible names and last initials both male and female that could have appeared above mine, what are the chances of it being Daniel M? There was a Daniel below me in number 8 as well, but the last initial was an R.

All of this happened within seconds. I had the idea to ask for the sign, and when I looked up there it was. There was no effort involved. It was like a game. Maybe Danny had it planned all along and had merely influenced my thoughts at the right time so that I would be able to look up and experience this. I don't begin to know how he managed to get that Daniel M up there.

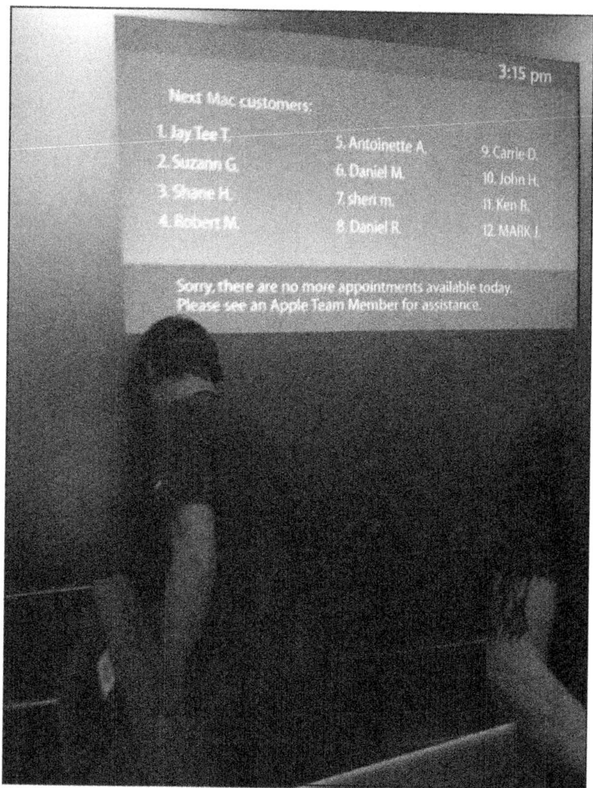

Here is the photo of the screen at *The Apple Store.*
Notice numbers 6 and 7.

I was so excited that I quickly grabbed my handy little iPhone and began snapping pictures of the blue screen before those two names had been replaced by others. Above is the photograph that I took at *The Apple Store.*

Connecting-Up

CHAPTER SIXTEEN

Can Anyone Connect Up?—Your Imagination May Be More Than You Think

I believe that we can all connect-up and that we often do without even realizing it. I also believe that connecting-up has more to do with paying attention to what passes through our minds and trusting what we feel than anything else.

Ever since the day after Danny passed, I heard thoughts that I believed were coming from him. These thoughts usually started out by referring to me as mom or Sheri (Dan was fond of calling me by my first name), and they sounded something like this: "Mom, I'm okay and I'm right here with you," to which I would think, "Sure Dan, that's nice and this is just my imagination!" Initially, I dismissed all of these thoughts as imagination. Nonetheless, the thoughts kept occurring. Whenever I felt really down in the dumps, I would be flooded by these loving and comforting thoughts which would lift my heart momentarily, until I dismissed them all as imagination. Then one day while I was dismissing some thoughts as imagination I heard, "Well Sheri, what do you think imagination is? Where do the imagined thoughts come from, did you ever think of that?" No, I guess I hadn't, but I knew I would now.

I now believe that thoughts do enter our consciousness that have been directed to us from spirit but it's hard to recognize them or to distinguish them from our own wishful thinking. I had never really thought about it, but I guess I expected spirit messages to sound ghostly or other-worldly. I certainly didn't think I'd be hearing a message in my own voice: however, that is the way it comes through. Medium Glenn Dove has told me that he hears the messages in his own voice as well. I think that I may "hear" the messages through some internal process that I am not aware of. By the time the thought occurs to me it seems to me that I'm just having a thought of my own and that it's nothing more definitive than that.

But as I started paying closer attention to these thoughts that did come through I had to laugh out loud, for in his inimitable way, Danny was teasing me. "Mom, you are so dramatic" I would hear when I was beginning to get emotional, or "Sheri, you're a gossip!" when I was telling a good story. It seemed to me as if I was getting a look at myself through Dan's perspective.

For this next section of the book, if you have not done so already, purchase a journal to start keeping a record of the thoughts, feelings and ideas that come to you. So much comes through that is lost if not documented. I know that at first it isn't easy to trust the origins of what you hear to anything beyond your own imagination, but then I ask you, how can you define the scope and reach of imagination? I refer you to this quote by Albert Einstein:

> *Imagination is more important than knowledge. For knowledge is limited to all we now know and understand, while imagination embraces the entire world, and all there ever will be to know and understand.*
>
> —Albert Einstein

On April 22, 2011, I was sitting in my room, attempting to quiet my mind through meditation when I began to hear the following ideas. I hadn't experienced this in a long time, so I grabbed my journal and began writing what I heard. I think it belongs in this chapter. I call it, "More from Dan."

> It's been such a while since you have allowed me to do this... to run away with your thoughts and tell you how it is. And the reason for this is, of course, your doubts in the validity of what you hear.
>
> It's as simple as that. Doubt holds you back as it holds everyone back from trusting their own feelings and impulses. But truth be told I've been coming to you from the beginning and you were less reluctant to write this stuff up two years ago. The reason you are taking so long to get this book written is because you get so caught up in judging the material that you have days on end where you can't write at all. Just let it go. You hear it, write it. I won't betray you and your thoughts won't betray you either. You see, to be a medium takes that leap of trust as you call it because how is a medium to know the validity of what he or she hears? They don't know these people from Adam and they couldn't possibly know what is real for them, but they have a respect for what comes through and they verbalize it.
>
> The average, common person is more in touch with their departed loved ones than they ever suspect because we do come around, and of course, in the cases of so called lost children, we come around a great deal. But most people have that inner door very well sealed and ideas and information that flashes by in their minds is not seen for what it is, and therefore it is just wasted on them. Sometimes a parent is able to receive some of the energy that is placed around

them, but they will seldom attribute the lift as coming from spirit. You were always struck by the message I gave to Jess through that first billet reading with Reverend Ron in which I said, "Drink in the white light that is all around you." That wasn't just a pretty thing to say to my sister. I literally put white light around her when I visit her! We do put it around you, all of you. You're just so stuck in physical reality you don't believe it. Well, you do more than most mom, and that's why you are doing better than a lot of the parents you try to help. But things move slowly down on the earth. Look how long it has taken you to come this far and still, this is the first thing you have allowed me to do in terms of what you call Direct Communication in writing since July of 2008. I'm glad you're getting back to this. We have a lot to talk about.

But the first thing that you have to get into your thick skull and then spread it outward like butter on bread, is that this is all real. Just because you can't see something with your physical eyes or hear it with your physical ears, or with any of your magnificent five senses, doesn't make it not so. We are as real today as we ever were before and we have been removed from your sight, but we are just not gone from your space. To sense our energy and to have this direct communication, you have to accept the reality of our existence and let what you cannot see penetrate into you from other means.

Of course there are ways to help people to get the ball rolling and I know you are trying to teach meditation as a way for people to begin to observe thoughts from a witness perspective, but none of this will work for them if they don't accept the possibility that this is real. You sit there, ever ready to ask, "Is this real?" so imagine how remote and distant and pie-brained this would seem to someone else who has had much less experience with this than you. So, step one is to open your mind to the possibility that we are real. The next step is to realize that your imagination is real. It draws upon what you don't see. What comes into your mind isn't just limited to your mind alone. Your mind is a doorway into all kinds of information that enters through a portal called imagination. So the thing to start doing is to observe what is going through your mind without dismissing it. Look at the images in your mind, listen to the thoughts you are thinking, write them down and let your imagination go with it, don't try to control it. People can develop this direct connection on their own and some have. Those people fare better because in fact, energy is exchanged, as well as ideas. We hear your thoughts and you can hear ours, however, most people dismiss everything they hear as imagination, so I ask you, "What do you think imagination is?" We'll leave it at that. That's an important question. So much comes your way through imagination. Think about it!

The true sign of intelligence is not knowledge but imagination.
—Albert Einstein

CHAPTER SEVENTEEN

Let's Connect Up—Getting Started

When close friends of ours lost their son in 1996, Jerry and I offered to write eulogies for the memorial service. Our friends asked their rabbi if he had any objections to us speaking. He told our friends that it was their decision but he requested that we try not to make anyone cry. Not make anyone cry?

If there was ever a time to cry, I felt this was it. I have always believed that crying is therapeutic and I feel sorry for the countless men whose tears were permanently dried up in their attempts to become men. The sky would never hold back its storms and perhaps it has better sense than we do, because after a good rain, the humidity is able to clear out again.

When you work with the following exercises you will feel emotions coming up. Some of you will be moved to cry. You may open up some well-guarded wounds. My opinion is that this is good because when you bottle up these feelings inside you, they don't go away but accumulate under the surface until one day they become overwhelming. Don't be afraid to feel and don't be afraid to cry. It clears out the humidity and allows for a brighter day to come.

If you recall, the last thing that Dan said was that the single most important thing needed to connect-up is a mind open to the possibility that he and all the others that we love on that side, exist. He was quite adamant that if your mind is completely closed to that possibility that you make it next to impossible to connect-up. Not because you can't get the messages but because you won't consider them valid and so they will have no meaning for you.

Our loved ones are around us and they will try to convey their thoughts and feelings to us, but as I said, these thoughts and feelings come in through the window of our own imagination and they are easy to miss or discredit. That said, let's get started.

The Ground Rule: Keep an Open Mind

We've already determined that the first most important component needed to connect-up is an open mind, however that doesn't mean that you need to have certainty about this. Doubts are a normal and natural part of a questioning mind. You do not have to have a doubtless mind. Keep in mind that faith does not imply certainty. On the contrary, faith involves a leap of trust into that which you cannot see, for if what we were talking about were seeable and self-evident, we would not need faith.

The Practice: Put Aside Time

Whether you do this everyday, a few times a week, or once a month, choose a place where you can relax and use Focused Breathing (outlined below), to quiet your mind and bring your focus into the present moment.

I always start with a Focused Breathing Meditation and there are many reasons for this. The first has to do with quieting down my noisy mind. I think we've all experienced being swept away by thoughts to such a degree that we were hardly present in the moment. As if addicted to the storyline in our own minds, we can go over and over the same thoughts, in much the same way that a monkey swings from branch to branch.

The focus on breath helps you to step aside from your familiar place in the middle of your thoughts, often referred to as "Monkey Mind" to become the observer. This process has been called "Cultivating The Witness."

A. Use a Focused Breathing Meditation Technique to Tame "Monkey Mind" and "Cultivate the Witness"

1 Start by finding a quiet place where you can sit or lie comfortably. If possible turn everything off that might distract you. Ideally you want to have a quiet space. I often use small wax earplugs to block out house noise and to magnify the sound of my breath.
2 Begin by inhaling and exhaling through your nose. (If you have a cold you can use your mouth.) Now focus all your awareness on the tip of your nose, (if you are using your mouth focus your attention on the inside of your lips) and imagine that you are the gatekeeper at the gates of a big city and that it is your very important job to watch the coming and going of your breath.
3 Focus solely on your breath and feel it as it passes in and out of your nostrils. As you breathe in think, "I am breathing in cool" and as you breathe out think, "I am breathing out warm." Feel the cool air as it enters your nostrils and the warm air as it leaves you. "Breathing in cool, breathing out warm. Breathing in cool, breathing out warm. In cool, out warm. In cool, out warm." Try to maintain your focus on the breath.
4 Inevitably your mind will wander. This is normal and common. Most people find that their minds wander off constantly. Like a monkey swinging from branch to branch, your mind may swing from one thought into another.

Here is an example of how the mind can wander: "What did she say? I can't remember. It had something to do with the dog. Did I remember to give the dog water? Damn, this isn't working! I'm supposed to be breathing. I can never do anything right. Did I remember to give the dog water?"

On and on your mind will wander off. As soon as you realize that you have lost the awareness of your breath, as if you were training a puppy, gently lead your mind back to your breathing. Again and again your mind will wander off. Again and again you will return yourself to the breath.

5 "Breathing in cool, breathing out warm. Breathing in cool, breathing out warm. In cool, out warm. In cool, out warm." The main idea is to stay with the breath until you become aware that your mind has wandered off into thought. Once you realize that your mind has wandered, you gently bring yourself back to breath.

Most of the time my experience entails me breathing, me thinking, me catching myself lost in thought and then me returning to the breath. Over and over I catch myself lost in thought, over and over I return to the breath. "In cool, out warm—in cool, out warm. For the longest time I couldn't figure out what interspersing this breath between my thoughts was possibly doing for me. One day, however, I came to see that each time I caught myself lost in thought and opted to return to the breath, that I was stepping back from inside the thoughts, backing off from my usual position in the middle of my thinking mind to a position where I could breathe more calmly and observe my mind as if the witness to it.

Sometimes I am surprised at what I see, sometimes I am upset, sometimes I am touched, but I am always curious because I've learned so much about myself and mixed in with all those other thoughts are the thoughts that sound more like Dan's than mine. It's as if I am observing my own mind from a new perspective.

This isn't always easy because sometimes you see that you have thoughts that are downright mean. This meditation technique provides a bird's eye view of how you think and talk to yourself so you will see a lot about the workings of your own mind. If you stay with this, after a while you will observe that certain thoughts come up habitually. You will also observe that you spend a lot of time daydreaming. Jot down what you observe when you go back to the breath.

At this point in the meditation keep your journal nearby to record the thoughts and ideas that come to you. If you see something coming up time and again in your mind, jot it down. If you have a thought about your loved one, write it down. If an image comes to you, record it. In a sense, you are observing the laboratory of your own mind whose reaches we will not limit to the here and now.

As I've said before, I don't actually know how or when these messages come through. Something must take place on another level of consciousness that I am completely unaware of because when the thoughts occur to me, they seem to be ordinary, common thoughts or everyday daydreams. That is why I say it's a matter of trusting the thoughts that make it through to you, because they do come through. Even if we are not aware of how and when it happens, they do come through.

I want to make it very clear that when I get messages from Danny they come in through that window of imagination. There was absolutely nothing extraordinary about the thoughts and it is only because I was paying attention to them, jotting them down and then investigating them through mediums and signs that I came to see that they were more than just a daydream in my mind.

Use Focused Breathing Meditation to step back, relax and

observe your mind. Keep a journal nearby to document your thoughts and feelings.

B. Initiating Conversation

You can initiate conversation by simply asking your loved one a question. While continuing with Focused Breathing just think the question in your mind and observe what comes up. Keep a record because it is easy to forget what comes to mind when you are meditating, and the information often makes more sense over time.

Keep in mind that whether you sense any response or not, that your loved one can hear you, so continue the conversation by expressing your feelings. A one way conversation is still better than no conversation at all, for it can be very healing to mentally express your innermost feelings. If you are carrying regrets about something, say it. If you just want to express your continued love, then do so. Begin the process of opening up and mentally talking to your loved one because it initiates the conversation.

Begin connecting-up with your loved one by directing thoughts out to him or her and then observe the feelings and thoughts that come back to you. Remember that signs can show up in numerous forms, from songs on the radio to a boat like the Free Bird sitting on the Hudson River, to the impulse I had to look out at the river at precisely the right time to see the boat. So be open to them in whatever form they come in and keep a record of it all.

C. Characterized Breathing—Adding Visualization to the Breath

The next step, which adds visualization to the breathing technique, strengthens your focus on breath and assists you in absorbing and directing energy. I learned the technique of Characterized

Breathing from the great British spiritual healer Harry Edwards. Harry explained that by adding visualization to the breath you literally make it possible to draw energy into yourself from forces that are around you. I always combine Focused and Characterized Breathing when working with energy. I use it as a means to absorb energy and to direct it in numerous ways. After Danny passed I began to use this technique for sending out my love to him and drawing in his love to me. What I found is that it lifted me. (See The Love Infusion which follows.)

1 **FILLING YOURSELF WITH ENERGY:** Continue with your breathing, focusing on the feeling of the breath as it enters and leaves your nostrils. This time as you inhale, feeling the cool air, visualize streams of energy entering into you. You can see this as golden light as I do or use whatever image pleases you, however, in your mind's eye imagine that you are drawing cool, healing energy into you. Simply draw breath into you and as you do think, "I am breathing in cool, light healing energy into me." As you exhale, allow your body to relax and release any tensions that you may be holding and think, "As I exhale I am releasing all stress from my body." And again, inhale and as you do think, "Inhaling I am drawing cool healing energy into me," and as you exhale think, "Exhaling I release all the tension I am holding in my body, relaxing and letting go." Repeat this step until you feel a bit more relaxed and ready to move on.

Now inhale again, continuing to envision streams of healing energy entering into you. This time as you exhale imagine the energy flowing into your body and filling your body with light and healing energy. When you inhale think, "Breathing in I draw light and healing energy into me." As you exhale think, "Breathing out I direct this energy into my body. I am filling my body with light and healing energy." As you breathe in, draw the energy into you. As you exhale, direct this energy into your body. Envision it moving through your arms right out to your fingertips, down through your legs, and out to the tips of your toes. Repeat this step until you feel sufficiently energized.

2 **DIRECTING THE ENERGY INTO YOUR HANDS:** Continue to use Characterized and Focused Breathing to direct energy into your hands. Continue with your breathing inhaling deeply and fully, while at the same time envisioning drawing streams of healing energy into you. This time, as you exhale, envision this energy entering into your hands and charging them with healing energy. As you inhale think, "Breathing in, I draw light and healing energy into me." As you exhale think, "Breathing out, I direct this energy into my hands. Breathing in I draw cool healing energy into me. Breathing out I direct this warm healing energy into my hands." Repeat this step until you begin to feel warmth in your hands.

Now, place your hands on your body anywhere that you desire to receive this healing. You can place your hands on your heart for emotional healing. As you inhale you visualize as well as think "I am drawing healing energy into me." As you exhale you visualize and think, "I am directing this energy into my hands and from my hands into my body." Repeat this step until you can feel the warmth from your hands entering your body.

Practice this numerous times until it becomes second nature. In time you will begin to feel heat in your hands, and if you stay with this practice, you will be able to effectively use your hands for healing.

D. The Love Infusion, Sending Out and Drawing In: An Energy Exchange With Spirit

Use Focused and Characterized Breathing to inhale deeply and fully and to exhale thoroughly. Now envision your loved one here with you in any way that you like. I visualize Danny standing at the foot of my bed, about three feet away from me, but how you want to picture this is totally up to you. Continue to use your breathing technique. Inhale deeply and fully, envisioning streams of healing energy entering into you. This time, as you exhale and feel the warm air passing out of the tip of your nostrils, imagine sending that energy out from you to your loved one. As you breathe in you think, "I am inhaling cool healing energy into me." As you exhale you think, "I am sending this healing energy and love outward to you." Do this again: "Breathing in I draw this energy into me. Breathing out I send all of my love and energy out to you."

ADDING DIALOGUE: Continue with your breathing technique and draw energy into you as you inhale. On the exhale, as you envision sending this energy to your loved one you mentally say, "I love you, I love you, I send you this love." Say it over and over until you have emptied out all the air in your lungs. Now, use your imagination to help you envision your loved one speaking those same or similar words to you as you inhale. Breathe in deeply and fully, and as you do this envision drawing love and energy into you as you repeat the same words now coming from your loved one to you: "I love you, I love you, I send you this love." Breathe it in. Keep repeating the words and the visualization until you have inhaled all the air possible into your lungs. Continue to repeat these words coordinating them with the in-breath and the out-breath. You will find that it is easy to work with the out breath because you are expressing the love that you feel and that comes naturally. It takes a little more trust to draw the breath in, but stay with it because energy is exchanged. The fact is that your loved ones are close but invisible to you. Keep in mind that their invisibility does not prevent a valid energy exchange from taking place, from which you will emerge feeling a little stronger and a little bit better. Even if it were merely a figment of your imagination it would be energizing, however, there is no question in my mind that energy is exchanged.

E. Connecting-Up Through Dreams: Using Suggestion to Program Your Dreams

When I was a kid I would wake up in the morning with a long dream sequence in my mind. At the time I thought of my dreams as mere cartoons and so I wasn't particularly impressed. Now I believe that dreams contain all kinds of valuable information, but my recall is not nearly as good as it used to be. I find that it helps if I tell myself that when I wake up I will remember my dreams and so I use suggestion as I am falling asleep.

I had a teacher named Seth, who referred to physical reality as Framework 1 and non-physical reality as Framework 2 and I think this is a helpful analogy. From this perspective, our bodies and our waking experience all exist in Framework 1, but we spend a good portion of that time sleeping and dreaming, and in our dreams our consciousness enters Framework 2, which I've come to think of as the invisible counterpart to Framework 1.

I now believe that Framework 2 is a very valid state of existence. Our loved ones on the other side exist in Framework 2. I believe we go in and out of Framework 2 in our nightly dreams and in our daydreams as well. When people have near-death experiences they have entered into Framework 2. Prayer exists in Framework 2. Thoughts, feelings and emotions exist in Framework 2 along with all those things that you cannot see.

I believe that we are all sojourners into Framework 2, both in our dreams and in our waking experience, however, we are unaware of it. We all can remember times when we just knew something although we didn't know how we knew it. People will say, "I just have a gut feeling about this." Could it be that part of our consciousness interacts on other levels of reality and feeds information back to us in the form of feelings, images and thoughts? That's exactly what I believe happens all the time. An everyday example of this is when you think of someone and a minute later they ring your phone. Did that person send out a mental heads-up first? How did you pick up on it? You see, we don't know how we do it, but most of us do it all the time.

Radio waves and television waves are invisible. Because they can be picked up by receivers and translated into sounds and pictures we accept that they exist. In a sense, a good medium is like a finely tuned receiver for picking up and translating invisible thoughts, images and feelings directed from spirit; however, we can do it too. We all have the wireless mechanism built in. You can initiate connecting-up at any time, however you have to be willing to accept a relationship that is built on communication through feelings, thoughts, images and dreams.

Paying more attention to your dreams and keeping a dream journal can open up another viable window of communication; however, if you think of your dreams as a bunch of silly cartoons, they will have no meaning for you. Keep in mind that you will not find your loved ones in Framework 1. We have to seek them where they dwell.

We can't change the fact that they are on the other side and we are here. It's as if there is an invisible veil that sections us off from each other. But like gauze or cheesecloth, that veil is porous and cannot prevent love, energy, thoughts, feelings and images from penetrating it. It happens all the time. We just have to start paying attention to what comes through because somehow the ideas do get through.

The ball's in your court, and you've got all the tools you need, but it's up to you to step up to the plate and get that ball into motion. Keep in mind that you can modify the meditations in any way that makes them more useful to you. They are simply guidelines to get you started in quieting your mind and looking inward.

Inspiration and grace come from being quiet and letting your higher self speak to you.

It's hard to do that in this day and age when we are constantly being bombarded with noise. We have TVs running in the background as we have dinner or read, music playing while we are at the computer or iPods blasting as we work out. It is almost as if we are afraid of the silence.

Silence is the nucleus of the path to reaching our loved ones who cannot break through our shield of noise.

Standing in the middle of grief is in many ways the opposite of quiet. Even though we might be uncharacteristically quiet in the beginning, our minds are in constant motion going over the time we had together, or all the time we could have had promoting "our plans" for our child's future.

Our souls speak wisely, but oh so softly. We have to be centered, alert, still and poised for insight. Meditation does that, quiets the mind and empties it of random thoughts.

If we sit or lay still, we can follow our breath and the slow constant beat of our heart which is a drum beating out a call to our loved ones: "We are totally present, waiting to receive your grace."

—Vicky Bates

CHAPTER EIGHTEEN

Keep It Light—Keep Them Close—Keep It Going—Acknowledge the Elephant in the Room and Set Him a Place at the Table

I think we will all go a lot further with this if we keep it light and try not to be too serious about it. In a very real sense we are learning a new language: one that uses thoughts, images and feelings to communicate. Messages are often cloaked in symbols that require interpretation. Glenn Dove told me that when he sees a balance scale, he knows it is indicating legal issues and if he sees flowers, it usually indicates a birthday. After a session with Glenn my friend Susan Whelan remarked, "It's as if the spirits are holding up flash cards to Glenn" and I think that's a pretty good description of it.

When I asked Danny to "say Free Bird" to Roland and Roland came back with, "He says to tell you that he is as free as a bird and that he has finally gotten his wings," I was more than satisfied with the response. Someone else might be disappointed because technically, Roland did not say the words "Free Bird" but "free as a bird." Sometimes it takes a much bigger stretch than that, so you need to get your expectations out of the way and let the messages come into your imagination just as they do. Don't try to change what comes in to make it sound more rational or to fit your own ideas—just be open to what comes in and keep a journal.

Once you begin cultivating this relationship with your loved one, treasure it and keep it close to your heart. Every day you can acknowledge that he or she is close in spirit and send out your love. Take a minute to breathe in his or her love, and as you do you can say, "I know I can't see you but I believe that your love is all around me and I am breathing it into me now." Use Focused and Characterized Breathing to draw this energy into you and to direct it outward from you to your loved one.

Keep it going. Every day you can dedicate your efforts, whatever they may be, to your loved one. That can help you to imbue even the tiniest act with purpose. You can interact with your loved one by sending out thoughts and asking for a sign or an answer to your questions. Then it is wise, however, to back off and see what comes up. You may be driving in your car when you hear a song come on the radio that really speaks to you. Does that mean it's a message from your loved one? It's very possible.

On holidays and special occasions, set a place at the table or remember to make a toast for this person. Acknowledge the elephant in the room by bringing it right out into the open. If you're not afraid to talk about your loved one, friends and family won't be either. And if they are, at least you are setting the right example by putting your loved one front and center. I'm the first one to say: As Danny would have said, "It's all good" or in the words of Dan, "It's crazy." It makes me feel better and I know that the last thing Danny wants is for us to try to put him out of our minds.

In his book, *Raymond, or Life and Death,* the renowned British scientist Sir Oliver Lodge, chronicles his investigations into connecting-up with his son Raymond, who died on the battlefield during the First World War. Raymond communicated through many different mediums, clearly identifying himself to his father and siblings. The book is fascinating to read. I was particularly touched by this quote from Raymond Lodge:

"Father, tell mother she has her son with her all day on Christmas Day. There will be thousands of us back in the homes on that day, but the horrid part is that so many of the fellows don't get welcomed. Please keep a place for me. I must go now. Bless you again, father—Raymond."

I doubt that anyone saw Raymond sitting at the table that night at Christmas dinner, but I'd bet his family was less solemn than other bereaved families that Christmas because they understood that Raymond was there in spirit and that they were still a family. It's a far more livable perspective and a far more accurate one. Separated, but still connected by those feelings that make us human, we can find ways to keep in touch. And this is what I am talking about.

CHAPTER NINETEEN

Protect Yourself—Mary and Rose and Their Upsetting Experiences with Mediums

I think it's obvious that I love mediums and that I find the connection through an "Interstellar Telephone" to be one of the greatest sources of solace that there is. My concern however, is that as bereaved people we are especially vulnerable and need to be especially careful. The following two stories will illustrate what I am talking about.

The first story concerns my close friend Mary, who lost her twenty-five year old daughter Ginny to a case of Childhood Leukemia. Danny was still alive at the time but as I have always been interested in mediums and in communicating with my loved ones on the other side, I suggested to Mary that we explore different mediums together. I said, "Let's you and me go on a ghost hunt" and the idea appealed to her as well, so we were off and running.

The first mediums we went to see were Glenn Dove and Roland Comtois. Ginny always came through and reassured her mother that she was well and happy on the other side. She explained the choice that she had made on what she called a "soul level" to live a shorter life. In a session with Glenn Dove, Ginny came through and said, "I only needed a few semesters to finish up my masters."

In every session Mary attended, Ginny's message was the same: that it had been her time to pass, that she was very happy and that she was no longer ill or in pain. In one session she said that she was helping with children on her side, as well as keeping an eye on everyone at home. Naturally Mary was relieved after each session. Once Ginny came through and commented on the fact that Mary was wearing her fleece vest. This was true. Mary was wearing Ginny's fleece vest. Little things like that brought Mary a lot of comfort by demonstrating to her that Ginny was present with her now, even to the point of knowing what she was wearing that day. Looking back I can say that up until this point, the ghost hunt was going splendidly.

A few months later Mary came to me with the name of a medium in *New York City* that she was interested in seeing. The medium was highly recommended to her by a man she knew named Len. He was from our local hometown and had lost his teenage son to suicide approximately a year before. He had been going to this woman for over a year on a consistent basis and felt that she had helped his son greatly to work through some issues. "Sure" I said, "I'll go with you" and scheduled two back-to-back appointments.

I had the first appointment. I wasn't particularly impressed with my session, but I wasn't disturbed by it either. Mary's experience was quite different. Mary came out of her session terribly upset, crying in fact. I could not imagine what my friend had been told but it couldn't be anything good.

Arm in arm we left the office and I pressed Mary to explain what had taken place. Apparently, the medium told Mary that Ginny was very angry and very sad that she had passed so young and that she was having great difficulty making the adjustment.

She went on to tell Mary that she could help Ginny make this transition but she would need her to could come in for sessions on a regular basis, more like once a week or twice a month.

Boy was I glad that I was there! This was such an obvious case of someone trying to make a living and as I said to Mary, if this was the first medium we had tried to contact Ginny through, we might never have known differently. However, this was at least number five down the line on our medium list, and people like Glenn and Roland we had seen numerous times and this was the first time that we heard anything remotely like this. I could understand fully how this could have seduced Len, because especially in the case of suicide, it is easy to believe that there could be regrets, but in Ginny's case, it just didn't stack up. Nonetheless the damage was done.

In time Mary let it go. She realized how totally out of character the reading was, and she decided to disregard it, but if it had been her first reading, she might have gone down quite a rabbit hole. Always trust your own feelings about these things. If something sounds off base to you, than it most likely is. Our loved ones don't turn into totally different people after they pass. Personality survives death and it remains intact. Yes, most souls continue to evolve and grow after they pass over, but they are essentially themselves. If you don't recognize them at all, that should tell you something.

The second story concerns my friend Rose. She had an upsetting event in a session with a medium in upstate New York, close to where she lives. Her son Anthony was a young adult when he passed, a few years prior to this session. I had only known Rose for a short time when I received an email from her asking my opinion. "Have you ever heard anything like this before?" she asked, and proceeded to tell me about her session.

It was to be a thirty minute session. After twenty minutes had passed and Anthony's name was not yet mentioned, Rose got a little concerned. "I'm really here to connect with my son Anthony," she said to the medium, to which the medium replied, "Anthony doesn't want to talk to you. That is why he didn't come through. He said for you to go on with your life and to leave him alone!"

Rose was devastated and I was outraged. I have never, in all my years of experience, heard anything remotely like this. I emailed Rose and told her that in my opinion the medium was a fraud and a mean one too. For the first twenty minutes of the session she had not come up with one pertinent piece of information concerning Anthony and now she was coming up with this horrendous lie to explain why. Imagine the years of pain a remark like that could cause, if Rose chose to believe it.

I suggested that Rose make an appointment with Glenn Dove, who is gifted, affordable, and does private sessions both in his office on Long Island, or over the phone. Rose opted to take my advice and made an in-office appointment with Glenn. On that day Rose and her husband drove down from upstate N.Y.

On the day of the appointment, I was excited too. I had been reassuring Rose all along that Anthony would come through and clear up the whole mess. I hoped I was right. When I finally heard from Rose I could tell by the sound of her voice that she had had a good session. Anthony had come through with a very different message. He expressed his continued love for Rose and his interest in her art. He spoke of his existence now and said that he was doing well on the other side. He assured her that he stays close to her. It was day and night from the former reading.

I hate to think of the unnecessary pain and hurt that can be inflicted on the bereaved by those less than altruistic people and we all know that the world is full of them, so you must check out your mediums very carefully. And remember, if the session is not feeling right to you, if the medium is not making connections that make sense to you, you can stop a phone conversation or get up and walk out of a session at any time. It's *your* heart and *your* mind and you must always protect yourself. Of course any professional can have an off day, but with a good medium, identifying and evidential information should come through without you having to say a word.

CHAPTER TWENTY

The Importance of Trusting Your Own Feelings and Validating Your Own Experience

For all of us who believe that personality survives death there will be at least ten times as many people who don't and many others on the fence. There are many religions that speak of an afterlife, but strictly forbid their constituents from connecting-up. Non-believers will find explanations for anything you share with them, no matter how evidential, ranging from fraud to coincidence.

I have come to accept the fact that there are people who will always find someone like me nutty. They just can't get on board with what they have categorized as spiritual hocus-pocus. I understand that. I used to feel that way too until the "real world" had failed me so pitifully that I had to stretch the horizons of what I knew in order to heal. For many of us, it takes a desperate situation to bring us to a place where we are really willing to open up new doors. Losing someone you love very much is one of those situations.

For parents it is next to impossible to break the habit of parental concern. It's very hard to see a child go over and then just put it to bed. You're still a parent with all the built-in instincts of protection. It is the most natural thing in the world to want to know where your child is and if he or she is okay. This ongoing love and concern never ends.

If you begin your own investigation into connecting-up, I have no doubt that you will get some interesting results, though it will be up to you whether you just dismiss all of it, or take it seriously. If a thought occurs to you, be brave enough to write it down. If a whole bunch of ideas come to you, make a note of them. If you asked your loved one for some direction and an answer comes to you in the form of a song or a caption on a billboard, say thank you and remember to make a note of it.

You begin by accepting the premise that your loved one in spirit is near and can hear you, and then you start cultivating a relationship through thoughts, images and feelings. You bring your loved one to mind in a positive way and you take a moment every day for sending out and breathing in the love.

Understand that it is totally up to you whether you believe or disbelieve in what you are doing. It's a very internal relationship. You're not going to see or hear your loved one. Most of the time, I'm not even aware of any exchange that is taking place between Danny and me. I either just know something, like gut-feeling knowing, or the words enter my head as if I'm talking to myself. As I have said before, it's such a subtle whisper that it's easy to disregard it. If you don't begin to trust in yourself as well as in the existence of your loved one, you will not gain much satisfaction from connecting-up in this way. But, if you will begin to trust what comes through and if you are willing to accept the possibility that it could be real, it grows in depth and scope and you begin to feel closer and closer to your loved one.

Today is August 27, 2011. Sitting here typing this, I am waiting and watching for Hurricane Irene to arrive, bringing storm conditions that threaten to flood the area and shut off the power. As I was looking for candles and flashlights I remembered a power outage we had when Danny was about six years old. It lasted for about five days and Dan was enthralled with the entire situation. His older brother was sick with the flu so Danny was my right hand man and he enjoyed every minute of it. As soon as he got off the school bus and into the house he would start rounding up candles and flashlights for when the sun went down. He helped me heat and serve dinner to Aaron and he didn't even miss the television. He was in a world of his own. On the day he got off the school bus to find that the power had been restored, he was visibly depressed.

These memories were so nostalgic that they brought me back to that place of longing: "If Danny were here, he would love this. If Danny were here, he would do this. If Danny were here, he'd be taking care of me." A second later in my mind I hear, "I am here with you. What do you think? Do you really think I would miss this?"

At this point my spirits have been lifted so much by this inner relationship that Danny and I share, that even if this was just an imaginary relationship I would still be better off. However, everything in my experience tells me that the reason I feel better is because there is an ongoing energy exchange that takes place between Danny and me and it helps me to cope with his departure from physical reality. I smile a little easier, I laugh a little heartier, and I don't feel the same bitter sting of loss.

Connecting-up will not heal all the wounds of loss. There is an opportunity for communication, but we all know that we have lost something significant. I do not need to list all the unfulfilled possibilities that we mourn. But to be in communication, to be able to still be in touch is infinitely better than living in a state of total loss. True, I've lost Danny to the world of flesh, but I've found Danny in the world of spirit and it is my best and only solace.

CHAPTER TWENTY-ONE

Conclusions and Final Words From Dan

In conclusion there are a few things that I have learned from these communications that were not mentioned in the book thus far. I would like to mention them now because I think they are important.

From all I have learned, the spirit realm is full of support. No one passes alone. Even if a child passes prior to his or her parents or anyone he or she knew in life, someone familiar will be on call to assist them.

When you cross over, no matter what your issues were, you will be given help and guidance and there is nothing to fear.

There is no hell or purgatory as we think of it. Instead, there is compassion and understanding. Dan specifically wanted me to say to all of those who have lost loved ones to suicide, that even those who took their own lives make it to heaven!

He wanted me to say that they are all there and that they are all okay and that we can all lighten up a little bit.

On a completely different note, you do not need to meditate to connect-up. It's a helpful tool, but it is not a requirement. Sometimes in the heat of an event, spirit intervenes. Many times when

Dan has come through, I was not in a meditative state at all. I teach it because it is what I do when I want to initiate spiritual connections of any kind, however, if playing golf works better for you, by all means play golf.

Once I understood how present Dan was and how my entire spiritual entourage on that side can see me, it made me want to do better for them. It's now about including them, not trying to get on without them. As a result, death isn't quite as horrific as I had once thought. If Dan's consciousness had been annihilated, leaving no trace of him intact, that would be unbearable. I feel for all the people who believe that is what happens when we pass.

On December 11, 2010 I was fortunate to take a workshop with Roland Comtois at *Star Visions* in Chappaqua, New York. The workshop focused on developing our ability to channel and there was extra time for Roland to channel and even for us to ask questions When it came to my turn to ask a question, I asked if Danny had a message for *The Prayer Team*, which as you know consists of bereaved parents. This is what he said:

> "Tell them that I exist. Tell them that our hearts and our love go on. Tell them to look everywhere, every day without pain and without sadness. We are all in the holiest of healing light and love. Just know we are not gone."

I hope that Danny and I have led you to at least consider that possibility. You have everything to gain and nothing to lose, for I truly believe that what you have lost in the flesh, you can find in the spirit.

May all healing blessings be with you.

Sheri Perl
September 14, 2011

CPSIA information can be obtained
at www.ICGtesting.com
Printed in the USA
BVOW08s1503230617
487711BV00001B/23/P